Bucks County, Pennsylvania Church Records

of the

17th and 18th Centuries

Volume 4

F. Edward Wright

HERITAGE BOOKS
2021

HERITAGE BOOKS

AN IMPRINT OF HERITAGE BOOKS, INC.

Books, CDs, and more—Worldwide

For our listing of thousands of titles see our website
at
www.HeritageBooks.com

Published 2021 by
HERITAGE BOOKS, INC.
Publishing Division
5810 Ruatan Street
Berwyn Heights, Md. 20740

International Standard Book Number
Paperbound: 978-1-68034-510-0

CONTENTS

PREFACE

It is our intent to complete these volumes as a collection of church registers and pastoral records of births, marriages and deaths in Bucks County of the 17th and 18th Century.

Our goal in gathering material for this project was to aid the genealogist by providing a single source of records. We find that many do not know the religious affiliation of their ancestors or the specific church; they do not know if records exist or where to find the records, if they do exist. Hopefully we have made the quest much easier. In looking for the records of a church one is burdened by the variations in church names and townships used by the various repositories. We hope that our approach eliminates all of these stumbling blocks.

Of enormous help in preparing the German church records has been the extensive research performed by Dr. Charles Glatfelter in his published work, *Pastors and People, Volume 1, Pastors and Congregations*. We have referred to it in locating and identifying the German congregations.

Other societies and repositories whose records we researched include the Evangelical and Reformed Historical Society; the Friends Historical Society, Swarthmore; the Historical Society of Pennsylvania, Philadelphia; and Bucks County Historical Society.

INTRODUCTION

The settlers who first came to Bucks County after the granting of Penn's charter were, with few exceptions, Quakers. Their settlements were concentrated in the southeastern part of the county. By May of 1682 William Penn had sold 565,000 acres to about 500 persons. Of these purchasers, about 50 acquired acreage in Bucks County.[1] These persons (one was a woman, Sarah Woolman) were mostly Quakers from Great Britain, especially England. The first settlers selected land along the Delaware as far up as the falls. By 1712 the general boundary of settlers had advanced to Plumstead. The Welsh Friends reached Richland in 1710. Welsh Baptists soon followed into Hilltown and New Britain. Early Dutch settlers, purchased land in Bensalem Township in 1689, namely, Nicholas, Leonard, Johannes and Frederick Vandygrift. Although less dominant in Bucks County than in other counties of Pennsylvania their immigration into Bucks County was becoming significant in the 1720s. By the time the Germans arrived most of the southern and central part of the county was already claimed by the Quakers and others. They settled in the northern part of the county and in those parts of Bucks County which became Northampton and Lehigh counties.

SOCIETY OF FRIENDS (QUAKERS)

Falls Monthly Meeting

The first monthly meeting was held at the home of William Biles on May 13, 1683 in Falls Township. For a few years prior to this date they met at private homes and went to Burlington for business meetings. The minutes of the men's meeting state that there was a,

"Meeting held at William Biles house 2d day of the 3d month 1683. then held to wait upon the Lord for his wisdome to hear what should be offered in order to inspect into the affairs of the Church that all things might be kept therein sweet and Savory to the Lord and by our care over the Church helpfull in the Work of God and we whose names are as follow being then present thought it fit and necessary that a Monthly Meeting should be set up both of men and woemen for that purpose and that this meeting to be the first of the mens meetings after our arivall into these parts. The ffriends present William Yardley, James Harrison, Phineas Pemberton, William Biles, William Dark, Lyonell Brittanie, William Beaks."

Middletown Monthly Meeting

In 1684 Falls Monthly Meeting was split into two monthly meetings, Falls and Neshaminy (later Middletown). Buckingham was set off as a monthly meeting in 1720. By 1800 a total of eight meetings had been established in Bucks County, Falls, Middletown, Wrightstown, Buckingham, Bristol, Plumstead, Richland and Makefield.

Buckingham Monthly Meeting

Buckingham Meeting was established in 1701 for "the new settlers above Wrightstown to have a meeting for worship weekly among themselves and others that might think fit to visit them..." It became a monthly meeting in 1720.

Wrightstown Monthly Meeting

A meeting was established there in 1686 to accommodate the families of James Radcliff and John Chapman. A meeting house was built in 1721. In 1724 Wrightstown Preparative Meeting joined with Buckingham Monthly Meeting and the monthly meetings were then held alternately between the two locations until Wrightstown was set off as a monthly meeting in 1734. After that time the Buckingham Monthly Meeting was held alternately between Buckingham and Plumstead.

Bristol Meeting

Bristol Preparative Meeting was founded around 1704 and belonged to Falls Monthly Meeting until transferred to Middletown Monthly Meeting in 1788.

Plumstead Meeting

Friends first held meetings in Plumstead in 1727. It was a part of the Buckingham Monthly Meeting.

Makefield Monthly Meeting

This was a Preparative Meeting under Falls Monthly Meeting. The Friends of Makefield were allowed to hold a separate meeting during the winter months beginning in 1750. That year they were given permission to meet at Benjamin Taylor's and Benjamin Gilbert's. The Makefield Monthly Meeting was established in 1820, composed of Makefield and Newtown meetings and held alternately at the two locations.

Richland Monthly Meeting

The first Quakers settled at Richland around 1710; it was known then as the Great Swamp. They established a preparative meeting as part of Gwynedd Monthly Meeting. It remained a part of the Gwynedd Monthly Meeting until 1742 when it was established as a monthly meeting under the Quarterly Meeting held at Philadelphia.

Quaker Records

Many of the Quaker records in this book were based on the copies made by William J. Buck. Mr. Buck was assigned to transcribe the Quaker records of Bucks County by the Library Committee of the Historical Society of Pennsylvania in 1870. This he completed by December 10, 1870; he also included in his copying, Quakertown, New Jersey and Gwynedd Monthly Meeting of Montgomery County, Pennsylvania. The Falls records prior to 1700 were previously thought to be lost but were supplied to him by a copy held in a Quarterly Meeting book of records, covering the period, 1683 through 1715 with births as early as 1662. He later commented that he found the records singularly perfect, so far as births, marriages and deaths were concerned, with but two exceptions, "that of Falls meeting which was so fortunately supplied, and the marriage book of Richland Monthly Meeting, from 1742 to 1804, the existence of which could not be discovered."

In our series of church records we have abstracted selected items from the minutes. Certain subjects (e.g., the selection of the burying ground, building the meeting house, etc.) were not included in this effort. The wording has been changed for brevity and clarity. For example, the phrase, "having this day declared their intentions of takeing each other in marriage," has been abbreviated to "intend to marry."

Quaker Marriages

In the case of marriages, the minutes sometimes contained no additional genealogical information. Other times the fact that the bride was a widow or the membership of the groom in another meeting was evident only in the minutes. And still other times information on the marriage was entirely missing from the register and from the record of the marriage certificates. That the clerk failed to record marriages was a concern to the monthly meeting and specific instructions were given to appointed members to oversee that "the marriage was orderly accomplished," AND that it was recorded in the records. The typical steps in marrying began at the monthly meeting when the couple announced their intentions. At a subsequent meeting, usually the next meeting, the couple announced their continued intention and at a subsequent meeting the committee appointed to oversee the marriage reported the marriage had been orderly accomplished. If the bride had children by a previous marriage a committee was assigned to ensure that the children's rights were protected. The marriage usually took place within the jurisdiction of the bride's monthly meeting. If the groom were a member of another monthly meeting he was required to produce a certificate recommending him as a worthy member and verifying that he was clear of any marriage engagements. After the marriage the bride might request a certificate (of removal) to be sent to the groom's monthly meeting indicating that the couple was planning to live "within the compass" of his monthly meeting.

Disorderly marriages
The Friends used several different phrases to indicate that a member had married contrary to their Rules of Discipline. The terms, "disorderly marriages," "out going in marriage," "married out of the unity of Friends," and "married by a hireling minister" - are virtually synonymous.[2]

Comparison to Hinshaw
William Wade Hinshaw is well-know for his monumental efforts in compiling many of the Quaker records. Volume 2 of his series, *Encyclopedia of American Quaker Genealogy* included two Pennsylvania monthly meetings, Philadelphia and Falls.[3] In the preparation of this volume he was aided by Thomas W. Marshall and Walter C. Woodward. Marshall in his introduction, states that only those subjects having genealogical interest were incorporated. In comparing our compilations of the Falls Monthly Meeting contained in this book one will easily see that they omitted references to military service, fornication (usually alluding to pre-marital sex), marrying cousins, indebtedness, disagreements between two parties, and other situations. We have included the latter types of information.

BAPTISTS
Rev. Thomas Dungan led an small colony from Rhode Island to Bristol in Bucks County in 1682/84 and formed the Cold Spring Baptist Church. It disbanded in 1702. Prior to the disbandment of the Cold Spring group the Southampton Baptist Church was formed as a part of the Church at Pennepack. The Church at Pennepack agreed to the separation in 1746. Abstracts of marriages, births, deaths, baptisms and other information of genealogical interest are recorded in this series. Many of the Southampton group were other than Welsh; the Welsh were especially well established in New Britain and Hilltown. Records of the Hilltown Church from its beginning in 1782 have also survived and are included in this series.

GERMAN LUTHERAN AND REFORMED
A considerable number of Lutherans migrated from New York in 1723 into the Tulpehocken area. Shortly thereafter migrations began coming directly from Germany including many of the German Reformed. These German immigrants moved into the unsettled parts of the county to the north. Tohickon Church in Bedminster Township was probably the first.

Lower Milford (Trumbauer's, Swamp Reformed)
The congregations begin in the 1760s. An acre of the land of Andrew Trumbauer was conveyed to the church in 1766.
Lutheran pastors: Philip Rapp, ca. 1766-1771; Peter Niemeyer, 1771-ca.1783; Christian Espich, 1792-1793; and Frederick Geissenhainer, 1793-1797.
Reformed pastors: John Christopher Gobrecht, 1769 - 1770; John Theobald Faber, Sr., 1772-1774; John William Pythan, 1774-1775; Casper Wack, 1776-1781; John Theobald Faber, Sr., 1782-1786; Frederick William Van der Sloot, 1786 (August - October); John Michael Kern, 1787-1788; John William Ingold, 1788-1790; and Nicholas Pomp, 1790-1797.
Present day address: Christ Church, 101 North Main St., Trumbauersville.
Records: The Reformed registers, found among the books of Rev. B. F. Luckenbill, begin in 1769. The first page has been lost while the second page shows that there were nine sets of sponsors, indicating that the records of at least nine baptisms have been lost. The earliest births shown begin in 1772. These records were copied by Rev. A. S. Leiby and checked for accuracy by William J. Hinke. Leiby's original submission and Hinke's corrections are available at the Philip Schaff Library.

Neshaminy
On June 18, three Dutch Lutherans, Abraham, Barnet and Christian Van Horn, purchased an acre of land, as a society of "People Distinguished by the name of Lutherans ..." In his will, dated November 12, 1750, Bernard van Dieren described himself as minister of the Lutheran congregations of Neshaminy. [Glatfelter] The relatively small group met in houses and barns, never building a church on the acre of ground which became the Feaster burying ground at Rockville, two miles south of Richboro.

Nockamixon
The Lutheran congregation register was begun in 1766. The Reformed are mentioned in 1773 in the minutes of the coetus. By 1814 there was a union church here.
Lutheran pastors: Michael Enderlein, 1766-1770; possibly Philip Rapp, Frederick Miller, 1773-1774; Peter Ahl, 1789-1791; and Anthony Hecht, 1792-1794. Glatfelter states that Peter Niemeyer might have served the Lutheran congregation between 1774-1783.
Reformed pastors: Casper Wack, 1773-1786, possibly followed by Frederick Von der Sloot and John Mann.
Present day address: St. Luke's Lutheran Church, 1/2 mile west of Ferndale and St. Luke's United Church of Christ, Ferndale. [The union

was dissolved in 1976/1977.]
Records: The Reformed records begin in 1773 and have been translated by C. W. Unger in June 1940. These are available at Philip Schaff Library. Charles R. Roberts performed an earlier translation in 1923. Some of his variations are shown in brackets in this book.
Lutheran Records: These records begin in 1766 and have been translated by William J. Hinke.

Ridge Valley
Land was sold for the location of a Union church in 1792.
Location: St. John's Lutheran Church, 1207 Allentown Road, Sellersville; Ridge Valley United Church of Christ, Sellersville.

Scheutz's (Great Swamp)
Milford Township
It was begun in the 1730s. It continued as the Great Swamp Union church in Lower Milford Township, Lehigh County for about its first 30 years. In 1762 or 1763 the Lutherans left and built a church 1 to 2 miles across the county line on land owned by Elder Lewis Schuetz.
Pastors: Frederick Reiss, 1756-1764; Peter Niemeyer, 1764-1771; Conrad Roeller, 1772-1775; John Schwarbach, 1776-1786; Carl Danapfel, 1789-1790; Christian Espich, 1790-1793; and Frederick Geissenhainer, 1793-1808.
Location: St. John's Lutheran, Route 663, 1/2 mile west of Spinnerstown.
Records: The earliest existing register begins in the 1800s.

Springfield (Trinity Union)
Springfield Township
The Reformed congregation was established in the 1740s and the Lutherans ca. 1751.
Lutheran pastors: Ludolph Schrenck, 1751-1754; Andrew Friderichs, 1754-1762; Otto Haase, 1763-1771; Christian Streit, 1772-1774; Peter Niemeyer, 1774-1783; Carl Friderick, 1784-1787; Peter Ahl, 1788-1790; and Anthony Hecht, 1791-1794.
Reformed pastors: John Conrad Wirtz, 1745-1749; Jacob Riess, 1760-1766; Egidius Hecker, 1766-1767; John Daniel Gros, 1770-1773; William Ingold, 1780-1781; Casper Wack, 1781-1786; Herman Wynckhaus, 1786-1790; John Mann, ca. 1792?; and Henry Hoffmeier, 1793.
Locations: Trinity Lutheran, 1/2 mile north of Pleasant Valley, on Route 212 and Trinity United Church of Christ, near Pleasant Valley.
Records: Lutheran records begin in 1751 (translated by William J. Hinke in 1927). The Reformed register begins in 1760 (translated by Hinke in 1921).

Tinicum
Bedminster Township
The Lutheran register begins ca. 1760. The Reformed congregation may have been established as early as 1789. The union began as early as 1808.
Glatfelter gives a tentative list of pastors: Lutheran - Wolfgang Leitzel, Frederick Miller, Peter Niemeyer, Peter Ahl and Anthony Hecht; and Reformed - Frederick Von der Sloot and John Mann.
Locations: Christ Lutheran Church, 2 miles east of Pipersville and United Church of Christ, Tinicum, Pipersville.

Tohickon Union
The congregations began in the late 1740s. The first church was built in Rockhill Township; a later church was built across the road in Bedminster Township.
Lutheran pastors: Martin Schaeffer, 1750-1753; Jacob Schertlin, 1754-1755; Joseph Roth, 1755-1758; Wolfgang Leitzel, 1760-1765; Philip Rapp, 1765-1773; and Conrad Roeller, 1774-1795.
Reformed pastors: Conrad Wirtz Gobrecht, 1766-1770; Casper Wack, 1771-1781; Theobald Faber, 1782-1786; Michael Kern, 1787-1788; William Ingold, 1788-1790; and Nicholas Pomp, 1790-1797.
Locations: Peace Lutheran Church, Hagersville, 3 miles north of Perkasie and St, Peter's United Church of Christ, Bethlehem Road, Perkasie.
Records: The Reformed register was begun in 1749 and the Lutheran register was begun in 1750.

Tohickon Lutheran (Tohecka, Birkensee, Keller's)
Bedminster Township
This Lutheran congregation in Bedminster Township began in the 1740s. It is easily confused with the above union church located three and one-half miles to the southwest in the same township.
Pastors: Ludolph Schrenck, 1749-1751; Lucas Raus, 1751-1753; Frederick Schultz; Helfrich Schaum, 1754-1758; William Kurtz, 1758-1759; Conrad Walther, 1761; and Otto Haase, 1762-1764; Michael Enderlein, 1766-1770; Peter Niemeyer, 1774-1783; Anthony Hecht, 1784-1788, 1792-1794; and George Wichterman, 1791.
Location: St. Matthew's, Route 563, 8 miles northeast of Perkasie.
Records: Lucas Raus began a register in 1751. The earliest birth recorded is dated 1754.

DUTCH REFORMED

Southampton (Neshaminy and Bensalem) Dutch Reformed at Churchville

The Dutch Reformed preceded the German Reformed into Bucks County and settled along the Neshaminy Creek near what is now Churchville. In 1710 Paulus Van Vlecq, a Dutch Reformed pastor, organized a congregation in Neshaminy and Bensalem. He served for three years followed by a long period without a pastor. Pastors: Paulus Van Vlecq, 1710-1713; Peter Dorsius, 1737-1748; Jonathan Du Bois, 1752-1772; William Schenck, 1777-1780; Matthew Leydt, 1780-1783; Peter Stryker, 1788-1790; John C. Brush, 1795-1796; Jacob Larzelere, 1797-1820.
Location: Churchville.
Records: The register begins in 1710.

Northampton Dutch Reformed

A second congregation of Dutch Reformed was organized in the Neshaminy area and a church built in 1753.
Pastor: Jonathan Du Bois until his death in 1772 when the congregation joined the Dutch Reformed Church.
Location: Richboro, Northampton Township.

MENNONITES

The Mennonites established their first congregation in Bucks County in 1735 in the northwestern part of the county, known at the Swamp Church of Milford. Later a meeting house was built in Bedminster. In 1746 a church was given to the followers at the Deep Run settlement. In 1752 a log building was erected for worship in the northwestern part of New Britain. The Perkasie or Hilltown meeting house was built in 1753, Gehman's in Rockhill in 1773 and in Springfield ca. 1753/1765.
Records: There are no known records of birth, marriage or death.

ANGLICAN (Protestant Episcopal)

The Anglican Church came into existence at Burlington with Bristol included. St. James was established at Bristol in 1717. There are no known records prior to 1800.

METHODISTS

Captain Webb, of the British army, introduced Methodism into Bucks County when he preached at Bristol in 1771, enroute from New York to Philadelphia. Classes were formed after the Revolutionary War.

ROMAN CATHOLIC

There were German Catholics in Haycock and Nockamixon by the close of the Revolutionary War. Haycock (St. John the Baptist) is mentioned in St. Joseph's records as early as 1764 and in Goshenhoppen records at about the same time. The church was not fully organized until 1798. The parish included Bucks and Northampton counties until 1833. For early references to Catholics in Bucks County, see records of St. Joseph's (Philadelphia) and Goshenhoppen (Berks).

PRESBYTERIANS

Records for the Presbyterian churches of Tinicum (Red Hill) and Neshaminy (Hartsville) in Warwick Township have survived and are included in this series. In the Tinicum records baptisms begin in 1760. In the Neshaminy records marriages begin in 1788 and baptisms in 1788. Marriages of the Presbyterian Church at Churchville were published in *The Pennsylvania Archives*, Volume 9, Second Series. Ministers at Tinicum include Johann Wolff Lezel and Frederick Miller. Ministers at Neshaminy Presbyterian Church include William Tennent, Charles Beatty, Samuel Blair and others.

Notes

1. J. H. Battle, Ed. *History of Bucks County*. The Reprint Company, 1985. Originally published: 1887, Philadelphia, PA. Names and acreages are given of those person who locate the whole or a part of their lands in Bucks County.

2. The term priest was also used to indicate a minister of another denomination.

3. William Wade Hinshaw, Thomas Worth Marshall, compiler. *Encyclopedia Of American Quaker Genealogy*. Genealogical Publishing Company, 1969. Originally published: 1938, Ann Arbor.

BIBLIOGRAPHY

Battle, J. H. Ed. *History of Bucks County*. The Reprint Company, 1985. Originally published: 1887, Philadelphia, PA.

Bieber, Edmund Ellis. *History of Trinity Evangelical Lutheran Church of Springfield Twp. Bucks County, 1751-1953*. 1953.

Davis, William W. H. Edited by Warren S. Ely and John W. Jordan. *A Genealogical and Personal History of Bucks County, Pennsylvania*. Originally pub. as Vol. III of *History of Bucks County Pennsylvania*. 1905. Repr. by Genealogical Publishing Co., 1975.

Fisher, Allen S. *Lutheranism in Bucks County, 1734-1934*. Tinicum, PA, 1935.

Furey, Francis T. *The Goshenhoppen Registers, 1741-1819*. Originally pub. in Records of the American Catholic Historical Society of Philadelphia, in a series, beginning in 1886. Repr. Baltimore: Genealogical Publishing Co. (1984).

Glatfelter, Charles H. *Pastors and People*, Volume 1, Pastors and Congregations. Breinigsville, PA: The Pennsylvania German Society, 1980.

Green, Doron. *History of Bristol Borough*. 1911.

Hinke, William John, Ph.d., D.D. *A History Of The Tohickon Union Church, Bedminster Township, Bucks County Pennsylvania. With Copy of Church Records Reformed Congregation 1745-1869. Lutheran Congregation 1749-1840*. Meadville, PA: The Pennsylvania German Society.

Hinke, William J., Ph,. D., D.D. "Early History of Keller's Lutheran Church, Bedminster Township, Bucks County," *Collection of Papers read before Bucks County Historical Society*, Vol., pp. 363-378.

Hinshaw, William Wade and Thomas Worth Marshall, compiler. *Encyclopedia Of American Quaker Genealogy*. Genealogical Publishing Company, 1969. Originally published: 1938, Ann Arbor.

Humphry, John T. *Pennsylvania Births, Bucks County, 1682-1800*. Washington, D.C. Humphry Publications, 1993.

Myers, Albert Cook. *Irish Quakers into Pennsylvania*. 1902.

Pennsylvania Archives, Vol. IX, Second Series. 1895.

Reed, Dr. W. H. *Great Swamp Reformed Church Records, 1736-1822.* Translated from the original transcript by Dr. W. H. Reed, Norristown, Pa. 1906. Copied by J. Christie from a copy type-written by William Summers. Conshohocken, Pa. 1907.

Roberts, Charles R. *St. Luke's Zion Church, Ferndale, Nockamixon Township, 1773-1897.* Allentown, PA. 1923

Roberts, Clarence V. Assisted by Warren S. Ely. *Early Friends Families of Upper Bucks. With Some Account of Their Descendants.* Originally published 1925. Repr. by Genealogical Publishing Co., 1975.

Roberts, Ellwood. *Old Richland Families.* 1898.

Streng, Samuel. *The History of North and Southampton Reformed Church, Churchville, Pa.* 1885.

Turner, D. K. *Neshaminy Presbyterian Church.* 1876.

RECORDS OF NESHAMINY PRESBYTERIAN CHURCH OF WARWICK, HARTSVILLE 1788-1800

Baptisms

Jane, dau of Francis and Margaret Baird, bapt. 12 May 1788, b. 10 Mar 1788, Warwick.

Samuel W., son of Samuel and Elizabeth Hinds, bapt. 13 Jul 1788, b. 19 Dec 1787, Montgomery.

Jane, dau of William and Rebekah Walker, bapt. 13 Jul 1788, b. 27 May 1788, Warwick.

William, son of Robert and Sarah Jamison, bapt. 24 Aug 1788, b. 27 Jun 1788, Warwick.

Mary, dau of Joseph and [blank] Miller, bapt. 9 Nov 1788, b. [blank], Warminster.

Agnes, dau of James and Eleanor Brooks, bapt. 9 Nov 1788, b. 25 May 1785, Warrington.

Jane, dau of James and Eleanor Brooks, bapt. 9 Nov 1788, b. 29 Aug 1787 Dauphin Co.

Mary, dau of Charles and Mary McMighan, bapt. 7 Dec 1788, b. 18 Jul 1787, Warwick.

Rebekah, dau of Samuel and Margaret Polk, bapt. 14 Dec 1788, b. 7 May 1787, Warminster.

Jane, dau of Thomas and Mary Roney, bapt. 22 Feb 1789, b. 25 Aug 1786, Warrington.

Isabel, dau of Thomas and Mary Roney, bapt. 22 Feb 1789, b. 21 Oct 1788, Warrington.

Isabel, dau of James and Marian McEwen, bapt. 1 Mar 1789, b. 4 Dec 1788, Warwick.

Anne, dau of Robert and Sarah Shannon, bapt. 1 Mar 1789, b. 20 Dec 1788, Warwick.

James, son of Samuel and Margaret Polk, bapt. 22 Mar 1789, b. 26 Jan 1789, Warminster.

Julia Ann, dau of James and Agnes Kirk, bapt. 27 Mar 1789, b. 25 Jan 1789, New Britain.

Margaret, dau of Matthew and Elizabeth Hinds, bapt. 5 Apr 1789, b. 4 Nov 1788, Montgomery.

Mary, dau of Hugh and Jane Ramsey, bapt. 26 Apr 1789, b. 30 Dec 1788, Warwick.

Lydia, dau of Adam and Jane Kerr, bapt. 25 Apr 1789, b. 18 Mar 1789, Warwick.

Hannah, dau of John and Mary McDowell, bapt. 3 May 1789, b. 27 Dec 1788, Warminster.

Mary, dau of Hugh and Anne Bartley, bapt. 9 May 1789, b. 29 Jan 1789, Warrington.

Robert, son of James and Rachel Darrah, bapt. 9 May 1789, b. 8 Feb 1789, New Britain.

Thomas, son of John and Mary Weir, bapt. 9 May 1789, b. 8 Jan 1789, New Britain.

Thomas, son of Henry and Ann McKinstry, bapt. 17 May 1789, b. 10 Feb 1789, Buckingham.

Margaret, dau of Paul Jr. and Margaret Dowling (Dowlin), bapt. 14 Jun 1789, b 25 Nov 1788, Montgomery.

John Marshal, son of James and Jane Marshall, bapt. 20 Jun 1789, b. 15 Aug 1775, Warminster.

James, son of Robert and Jane Cummings, bapt. 20 Jun 1789, b. 6 Aug 1788, Warwick.

Mary, dau of John and Elizabeth Campbell, bapt. 12 Jul 1789, b. [blank], Wrightstown.

Rebekah, dau of Robert and Mary McKinstry, bapt. 28 Jul 1789, b. 18 May 1789, Buckingham.

Agnes, dau of William and Mary Brown, bapt. 9 Aug 1789, b. 10 May 1789, Warminster.

Ann, dau of Jacob and [blank] Pricker, bapt. 27 Sep 1789, b. 31 Jan 1789, Durham.

Thomas, son of Thomas and Rachel Sebring, bapt. 27 Sep 1789, b. 26 Oct 1781 Solebury.

Jonathan, son of Thomas and Rachel Sebring, bapt. 27 Sep 1789, b. 16 Aug 1783, Solebury.

William, son of Thomas and Rachel Sebring, bapt. 27 Sep 1789, b. 18 Apr 178 Solebury.

Eleanor, dau of Thomas and Rachel Sebring, bapt. 27 Sep 1789, b. 8 Aug 1789, Solebury.

Josiah S., son of Samuel and Margaret Mann, bapt. 11 Oct 1789, b. 2 Sep 1789, Horsham.

Margaret, dau of Elijah and Mary Stinson, bapt. 15 Oct 1789, b. 29 Aug 1789, Warminster.

Samuel, son of Stephen and Jemima Murray, bapt. 25 Oct 1789, b. 22 Aug 178 Warminster.

Samuel, son of John and Jane Taylor, bapt. 25 Oct 1789, b. 15 Aug 1789, Warwick.

James, son of John and [blank] Rankin, bapt. 31 Jan 1790, b. 29 Dec 1789, Warminster.

Ellenah, dau of Isaac and Elizabeth Craven, bapt. 4 Apr 1790, b. 7 Dec 1789, Warminster.

Isabella, dau of David and Agnes Richey, bapt. 4 Apr 1790, b. 26 Jan 1790, Warrington.

Elizabeth Harris, dau of [blank] and Elizabeth Reynolds, bapt. 4 Apr 1790, b. 19 Jul 1786, Moreland.

James S., son of John and Jane Todd, bapt. 21 Mar 1790, b. 28 Dec 1789, New Britain.

Harriet, dau of William and Catharine Scout, bapt. 2 May 1790, b. 10 Jan 1790, Moreland.

James, son of Herman and [blank] Vangant, bapt. 2 May 1790, b. 4 Mar 1790, Warminster.

Mary, dau of John and Mary Horner, bapt. 7 May 1790, b. 3 Apr 1790, Warminster.

Elizabeth, dau of Samuel and Elizabeth Bushel, bapt. 13 Jun 1790, b. 17 Mar 1790, Warrington.

Elizabeth, dau of Jacob and Elizabeth Carrell, bapt. 4 Jul 1790, b. 7 Mar 1790, Northampton.

William, son of John and Jane Carr, bapt. 18 Jul 1790, b. 12 Sep 1789, Warwick.

Mary, dau of Solomon and Isabel Hart, bapt. 15 Aug 1790, b. 23 May 1789, Warminster.

William, son of Adam Jr. and Frances Carr, bapt. 12 Sep 1790, b. 28 Mar 1790, Warminster.

Rebekah, dau of Robert and Jane Cummins, bapt. 18 Oct 1790, b. 10 Feb 1790, Warwick.

Robert, son of Samuel and Margaret Polk, bapt. 18 Oct 1790, b. 9 Sep 1790, Warminster.

William, son of Matthew and Elizabeth Hinds, bapt. 19 Dec 1790, b. 26 Jul 1790, Montgomery.

Mary, dau of Elijah and Mary Stinson, bapt. 1 Jan 1791, b. 7 Oct 1790, Warminster.

John, son of James and Eleanor Polk, bapt. 30 Jan 1791, b. 9 Nov 1790, Warwick.

Catharine, dau of William and Sarah Harvey, bapt. 20 Mar 1791, b. 26 Jan 1791, Warwick.

Thompson, of Hugh and Jane Ramsey, bapt. 28 Mar 1791, b. [blank], Warwick.

John, son of John and Elizabeth Johnson, bapt. 3 Apr 1791, b. 8 Nov 1790, Warminster.

Margaret, dau of Hugh and Anne Barclay, bapt. 3 Apr 1791, b. 14 Jan 1791, Warrington.

Nathan, son of Robert and Mary McKinstry, bapt. 9 May 1791, b. 20 Jan 1791,

Buckingham.

Anna, dau of Samuel and Margaret Mann, bapt. 3 Jul 1791, b. 17 May 1791, Horsham.

John, son of Thomas and [blank] Roney, bapt. 3 Jul 1791, b. 14 Nov 1790, Warrington.

John Emmery, son of Laurence and Catharine Emery, bapt. 22 Feb 1792, b. 13 Feb 1789, Warwick.

Elizabeth Emmery, dau of Laurence and Catharine Emery, bapt. 22 Feb 1792, b. 13 Apr 1791, Warwick.

Elizabeth, dau of Charles and Mary McMighan, bapt. 22 Feb 1792, b. 4 May 1791, Warwick.

Silas, son of Job and Lucretia Barton, bapt. 11 Mar 1792, b. 16 Oct 1771, Warwick.

Britta, dau of Job and Lucretia Barton, bapt. 11 Mar 1792, b. 31 Mar 1774, Warwick.

Lucretia Barton, dau of Thomas and Britta West, bapt. 15 Mar 1792, b. 22 Feb 1737, Warwick.

Thomas, son of David and Agnes Richey, bapt. 23 Mar 1792, b. 25 Dec 1791, New Britain.

John, son of Francis and Margaret Baird, bapt. 25 Mar 1792, b. 20 Feb 1792, Warwick.

Martha, dau of Elijah and Mary Stinson, bapt. 1 Apr 1792, b. 30 Jan 1792, Warwick.

Benjamin, son of Chriswell and Sarah Gardner, bapt. 2 Apr 1792, b. 27 Sep 1790, Northampton.

Robert H., son of James and Mary A. McEwen, bapt. 6 May 1792, b. 10 Dec 1791, Warwick.

Samuel, son of Giles and Anne Craven, bapt. 9 May 1792, b. 15 Jan 1790, Northampton.

Helena, dau of Giles and Anne Craven, bapt. 9 May 1792, b. 28 Jan 1792, Northampton.

Henry, son of James and Rachel Darrah, bapt. 13 May 1792, b. 11 Jan 1792, Warminster.

Josiah, son of Samuel and Margaret Polk, bapt. 22 Jul 1792, b. 4 Jun 1792, Warminster.

Arcturus, of John and Jane Todd, bapt. 19 Aug 1792, b. 29 Jun 1792, New Britain.

Rachel, dau of Charles and Sarah Jones, bapt. 9 Sep 1792, b. 26 Jan 1782, Warwick.

John, son of Charles and Sarah Jones, bapt. 9 Sep 1792, b. 6 Feb 1786, Warwick.

Mathew, son of William and Mary Brown, bapt. 30 Sep 1792, b. 31 Jul 1792,

Warwick.

Mary James, dau of [blank], bapt. 27 Oct 1792, b. 9 Oct 1791, Southampton.

Joseph, son of Jacob and [blank] Carrell, bapt. 29 Oct 1792, b. 1 Jun 1792, Southampton.

James, son of John and Mary Horner, bapt. 29 Oct 1792, b. 21 Sep 1792, Warminster.

Wm, son of William and [blank] Whittenham, bapt. May 1792, b. 3 Dec 1759, Warminster.

Rebekah Whittenham, dau of Thomas and Lydia Livezey, bapt. May 1792, b. 16 Apr 1764, Warwick.

Hannah, dau of Wm and Rebekah Whittenham, bapt. May 1792, b. 3 Aug 1784, Warrington.

Wm Jr., son of Wm and Rebekah Whittenham, bapt. May 1792, b. 5 Sep 1786, Warrington.

Rebekah Jr., dau of Wm and Rebekah Whittenham, bapt. May 1792, b. 26 May 1788, Warrington.

John, son of Wm and Rebekah Whittenham, bapt. May 1792, b. 21 May 1791, Warrington.

Thomas, son of Samuel and Mary Strahorn, bapt. 29 Oct 1792, b. 2 Nov 1791, Great Valley.

Mary, dau of John Jr. and Mary Mann, bapt. 16 Dec 1792, b. 30 Nov 1792, Warwick.

James A., son of Samuel and Margaret Mann, bapt. 23 Dec 1792, b. 23 Oct 1792, Horsham.

Samuel, son of Matthew and [blank] Hinds, bapt. 3 Feb 1793, b. [blank], Montgomery.

Septimus, of John and Phebe Tucker, bapt. 17 Mar 1793, b. 4 Oct 1766, Buckingham.

John, son of Evan and Margaret Lukens, bapt. 17 Mar 1793, b. 27 Jun 1765, Horsham.

Eleonora, dau of Evan and Margaret Lukens, bapt. 17 Mar 1793, b. 2 Feb 1770, Horsham.

Samuel, son of Samuel and Barbara Murray, bapt. 31 Mar 1793, b. 13 Dec 1781, Horsham.

Martha, dau of John and [blank] Hagaman, bapt. 31 Mar 1793, b. 25 Dec 1783, Northampton.

Hannah, dau of John and Barbara Hageman, bapt. 31 Mar 1793, b. 25 Feb 1785, Horsham.

Priscilla, dau of John and Barbara Hageman, bapt. 31 Mar 1793, b. 15 Jun 1787, Horsham.

Phoebe, dau of John and Barbara Hageman, bapt. 31 Mar 1793, b. 25 Sep 1789, Horsham.

Barbara, dau of John and Barbara Hageman, bapt. 31 Mar 1793, b. 19 Sep 1791, Horsham.

Christian, son of John and Barbara Hageman, bapt. 31 Mar 1793, b. 6 Sep 1792, Horsham.

Anne, dau of Henry and Anne McKinstry, bapt. 10 May 1793, b. 17 Sep 1792, Buckingham.

John, son of James and Mary Kirkpatrick, bapt. 16 Jun 1793, b. 5 Sep 1788, Warminster.

Sarah, dau of James and Mary Kirkpatrick, bapt. 16 Jun 1793, b. 8 Nov 1790, Warminster.

Abraham, son of Isaac and Elizabeth Craven, bapt. 7 Jul 1793, b. 8 Jun 1793, Warminster.

Martha, dau of Michael and Elizab. Williamson, bapt. 7 Jul 1793, b. 9 Nov 1792, Warminster.

Sarah, dau of Hugh and Mary McGoochin, bapt. 1 Aug 1793, b. 25 Jul 1793, Warrington.

Jane, dau of Hugh and Anne Barclay, bapt. 4 Aug 1793, b. 7 Apr 1793, Warrington.

Charlotte, dau of John and Elizabeth Johnson, bapt. 11 Aug 1793, b. 23 Mar 1793, Warminster.

Martha, dau of Adam and Frances Carr, bapt. 11 Aug 1793, b. 6 May 1793, Warminster.

Henry, son of Henry and Alice Veon, bapt. 22 Sep 1793, b. 13 Jun 1793, Warrington.

Mary, dau of William and Olympias Walker, bapt. 11 Nov 1793, b. 1 Mar 1789, Warrington.

John, son of William and Olympias Walker, bapt. 11 Nov 1793, b. 23 Jul 1787, Warrington.

Hannah, dau of Nathan and Olympias Strahorn, bapt. 11 Nov 1793, b. 8 Mar 1793, Cheltenham.

Anne, dau of John and Anne McDowell, bapt. 2 Feb 1794, b. 5 Sep 1793, Moreland.

Eleanor, dau of John and Jean Todd, bapt. 6 Apr 1794, b. 8 Feb 1794, Warwick.

Anne, dau of James and Jane Barclay, bapt. 13 Apr 1794, b. 15 Nov 1793, Warwick.

Matthew, son of Robert and Dorothy King, bapt. 13 Apr 1794, b. 17 Dec 1793, Warrington.

Mary, dau of Hugh and Jane Ramsey, bapt. 20 Apr 1794, b. 21 Mar 1793, East Nottingham.

Sarah, dau of Samuel and Margaret Mann, bapt. 23 Mar 1794, b. 29 Dec 1793, Horsham.

John, son of John Jr. and Mary Weir, bapt. 23 Mar 1794, b. 10 Dec 1793, New

Britain.

Robert, son of Robert and Mary McKinstry, 23 Mar 1794, b. 21 Nov 1793, Buckingham.

Thomas Clemens, son of [blank], bapt. 27 Apr 1794, b. 25 Dec 1761, Horsham.

Mary Clemens, dau of [blank], bapt. 27 Apr 1794, b. 14 Sep 1768, Horsham.

John, son of Jacob and Sarah Hufty, bapt. 27 Apr 1794, b. [blank], Warrington.

Priscilla, dau of John and Elizabeth Campbell, bapt. 15 Jun 1794, b. 17 Mar 1794, Northampton.

Mary, dau of Thomas and Mary Clemens, bapt. 15 Jun 1794, b. 5 Jan 1794, Horsham.

Priscilla, dau of Robert and Mary Wallace, bapt. 22 Jun 1794, b. 20 Jun 1793, Warwick.

Hugh, son of Francis and Margaret Baird, bapt. 3 Aug 1794, b. 11 May 1794, Warwick.

Jane, dau of Stephen and Jemima Murray, bapt. 12 Aug 1794, b. 12 May 1794, Warminster.

Eliza, dau of John and Mary Mann, bapt. 10 Oct 1794, b. 26 Aug 1794, Warwick.

Sophia, dau of James and Mary Kirkpatrick, bapt. 2 Nov 1794, b. 18 Jul 1794, Warminster.

Thomas, son of Giles and Anne Craven, bapt. 18 Dec 1794, b. 23 Jun 1794, Northampton.

Isabel, dau of Samuel and Margaret Polk, bapt. 1 Jan 1795, b. 8 Nov 1794, Warminster.

Anne Roberts, dau of [blank], bapt. 4 Jan 1795, b. [blank], Warwick.

John, son of John and Elizabeth Roney, bapt. 4 Jan 1795, b. 24 Nov 1764 (1784?), Warwick.

Rachel, dau of Robert and Frances Mearns, bapt. 11 Jan 1795, b. 28 Nov 1794, Warwick.

Maria, dau of John and Jane Carr, bapt. 27 Feb 1795, b. 8 Oct 1791, Warwick.

John, son of John and Jane Carr, bapt. 27 Feb 1795, b. 18 Nov 1793, Warwick.

John, son of Thomas Jr. and Margaret Craven, bapt. 5 Apr 1795, b. 13 Jan 1795, Warminster.

Anne, dau of William and Elizabeth Johnson, bapt. 3 May 1795, b. 1 Dec 1794, Moreland.

James, son of Michael and Elizab. Williamson, bapt. 3 May 1795, b. 19 Feb 1795, Warminster.

Jane, dau of Elijah and Mary Stinson, bapt. 8 May 1795, b. 8 Feb 1795, Warwick.

Hetty, dau of Herman and Alice Vansant, bapt. 30 Aug 1795, b. 8 Jul 1795, Warminster.

Elizabeth, dau of John and Mary Roney, bapt. 17 Oct 1795, b. 23 Jul 1795,

Warwick.

Amy, dau of Edward and Jane Malawn, bapt. 19 Oct 1795, b. 10 Mar 1795, Horsham.

William, son of John and Mary Horner, bapt. 24 Jan 1796, b. 16 Dec 1795, Warminster.

Hannah, dau of John and Mary Rankin, bapt. 24 Jan 1796, b. 13 Dec 1795, Warminster.

James, son of Francis and Margaret Baird, bapt. 17 Apr 1796, b. 27 Feb 1796, Warwick.

Jane, dau of John and Jane Todd, bapt. 17 Apr 1796, b. 16 Jan 1796, New Britain.

Samuel, son of Samuel and Mary McKinstry, bapt. 9 May 1796, b. 16 Mar 1796 Buckingham.

Samuel, son of Thomas and Mary Roney, bapt. 9 May 1796, b. 21 Aug 1795, Warrington.

Charles, son of Gideon and Elizabeth Prior, bapt. 9 May 1796, b. 5 Jun 1795, Warwick.

Margaret, dau of Joseph and Elizabeth Wright, bapt. 11 May 1796, b. 19 Jun 1795, Horsham.

James, son of Jonathan and Mary Rich, bapt. 22 May 1796, b. 10 Sep 1795, Plumstead.

Hugh, son of James and Elizabeth Adams, bapt. 26 Jun 1796, b. 11 Apr 1796, Northampton.

Robert, son of John and Elizabeth Campbell, bapt. 3 Jul 1796, b. 5 Apr 1796, Northampton.

Mary Wilson Ramsey, dau of William and Rebekah Ramsey, bapt. 10 Jul 1796, b. 20 Jun 1795, Warwick.

Benjamin S., son of John Jr. and Mary Mann, bapt. 18 Sep 1796, b. 18 May 1796, Warwick.

[blank], of William and Griselda Carnaghan, bapt. 12 Sep 1796, b. 13 Oct 1785 Warrington.

William, son of Robert and Mary Walker, bapt. 12 Sep 1796, b. 7 Oct 1795, Warrington.

Betsey W., dau of John and Elizabeth Johnson, bapt. 9 Oct 1796, b. 14 Aug 1796, Warminster.

John, son of Mathew and [blank] Hines, bapt. 9 Oct 1796, b. 11 Aug 1795, Plymouth.

Robert, son of John and Mary Weir, bapt. 14 Oct 1796, b. 29 Apr 1796, New Britain.

William, son of Robert and Mary McKinstry, bapt. 14 Oct 1796, b. 21 Jun 1796 New Britain.

Eliza, dau of Robert and Mary Wallace, bapt. 17 Oct 1796, b. 11 May 1796,

Warwick.

Jonathan Delany, son of [blank], bapt. 17 Oct 1796, b. 5 Feb 1772, Warminster.

James, son of John and Mary McDowell, bapt. 24 Sep 1796, b. 17 Jun 1796, Warminster.

John, son of Stephen and Jemima Murray, bapt. 19 Nov 1796, b. 25 Aug 1796, Warminster.

Maria, dau of Robert and Frances Mearns, bapt. 1 Jan 1797, b. 2 Nov 1796, Warwick.

Elizabeth, dau of Jonathan and Anne Delany, bapt. 6 May 1797, b. 16 Jan 1797, Warminster.

William A., son of William and Sarah Long, bapt. 23 Jun 1797, b. 28 Feb 1797, Warrington.

James, son of William and Mary McEwen, bapt. 9 Jul 1797, b. 3 Mar 1797, Warwick.

Robert, son of John and Jane Carr, bapt. 12 Aug 1797, b. 25 Sep 1796, Warwick.

Mary, dau of John and Rebekah Simpson, bapt. 17 Sep 1797, b. 11 Aug 1794, Whitemarsh.

Samuel, son of John and Rebekah Simpson, bapt. 17 Sep 1797, b. 4 Oct 1796, Whitemarsh.

Sarah, dau of John and Jane Taylor, bapt. 17 Sep 1797, b. 26 Jul 1797, Hatfield.

John, son of Robert and Mary Walker, bapt. 10 Nov 1797, b. 8 Feb 1797, Warrington.

Rebekah, dau of Thomas and Mary Clemens, bapt. 15 Oct 1797, b. 31 Jul 1797, Horsham.

Sarah, dau of James and Elizab. Adams, bapt. 18 Feb 1798, b. 20 Oct 1797, Northampton.

Robert, son of Thomas and Margaret Simpson, bapt. 1 Apr 1798, b. 21 Sep 1797, Buckingham.

Martha, dau of James and Mary Sample, bapt. 1 Apr 1798, b. 23 Sep 1797, Buckingham.

Eleanor, dau of Elijah and Mary Stinson, bapt. 22 Apr 1798, b. 28 Dec 1797, Warwick.

John, son of John and Jane Todd, bapt. 29 Apr 1798, b. 20 Mar 1798, New Britain.

John, son of William and Eliza Callen, bapt. 6 May 1798, b. 17 Feb 1798, Warminster.

John, son of Samuel and Margaret Polk, bapt. 14 May 1798, b. 31 Mar 1798, Warminster.

Mary Vandevander, dau of John and Eliza Vandevender, bapt. 27 May 1798, b. 13 Dec 1797, Warwick.

Robert, son of Francis and Margaret Baird, bapt. 27 May 1798, b. 12 Apr 1798, Warwick.

Hannah, dau of Samuel and Margaret Mann, bapt. 1 Jul 1798, b. 22 Apr 1798, Horsham.

William, son of George and Barbara Madera, bapt. 3 Jul 1798, b. 25 Jul 1794, Warrington.

Mary, dau of John and Mary Rankin, bapt. 19 Aug 1798, b. 19 Jul 1798, Warminster.

George, son of Wm and Rebecca Whittenham, bapt. 26 Aug 1798, b. 13 May 1798, Warrington.

Elizabeth, dau of William and Sarah Long, bapt. 30 Aug 1798, b. 22 Jun 1798, Warrington.

Margaret, dau of John and Martha Harvey, bapt. 29 Oct 1798, b. 21 Jun 1798, Warminster.

Hannah, dau of John and Rebecca Simpson, bapt. 12 Feb 1799, b. 23 Nov 1798, Whitemarsh.

Wm Henderson Long, son of John and Anna Long, bapt. 13 May 1799, b. 3 Mar 1799, Warrington.

Jacob, son of Joseph and Elizabeth Wright, bapt. 15 May 1799, b. 28 Jan 1797, Horsham.

Mary, dau of John and Mary Weir, bapt. 15 May 1799, b. 11 Feb 1799, New Britain.

Rachel, dau of Michael and [blank] Williamson, bapt. 2 Jun 1799, b. 3 Apr 1798, Southampton.

Sarah, dau of Stephen and Jemima Murray, bapt. 16 Jun 1799, b. 16 Jan 1799, Horsham.

Lydia M., dau of Samuel and Lilly Ray, bapt. 28 Jul 1799, b. 23 Mar 1799, Horsham.

Sarah, dau of Robert and Frances Mearns, bapt. 16 Aug 1799, b. 20 Apr 1799, Warwick.

Helena, dau of Jonathan and Anne Delany, bapt. 29 Sep 1799, b. 26 May 1799, Warminster.

John, son of John Jr. and Mary Mann, bapt. 9 Oct 1799, b. 2 Sep 1799, Warwick.

John, son of Giles and [blank] Craven, bapt. 13 Oct 1799, b. 29 Jul 1799, Northampton.

James, son of Robert and Mary McKinstry, bapt. 13 Oct 1799, b. 29 Apr 1799, New Britain.

Mary and Sarah, daus of George and Barbara Madera, bapt. 3 Jul 1798, b. 5 Mar 1798, Warrington.

Hannah, dau of Joseph and Elizabeth Wright, bapt. 15 May 1799, b. 4 Apr 1799, Horsham.

Isabel, dau of Robert and Mary Wallace, bapt. 28 Oct 1799, b. 15 May 1799, Warwick.

John, son of John and Mary Horner, bapt. 12 Jan 1800, b. 23 Oct 1799, Warminster.

Jane, dau of John and Mary Torrence, bapt. Oct 1799, b. 15 Mar 1797, Warrington.

William, son of John and Mary Torrence, bapt. Oct 1799, b. 16 May 1798, Warrington.

William, son of Isaac and Elizabeth Craven, bapt. 2 Feb 1800, b. 21 Nov 1799, Warminster.

John, son of Gideon and Elizabeth Prior, bapt. 6 Apr 1800, b. 21 Sep 1799, Warminster.

James McNiel, son of Daniel and Eunice McNiel, bapt. 11 Apr 1800, b. 8 Aug 1797, Buckingham.

Thomas McNeil, son of Daniel and Eunice McNiel, bapt. 11 Apr 1800, b. 28 Dec 1798, Buckingham.

Rachel Callen, adult, bapt. 15 Jun 1800, b. 21 Sep 1777, Warminster.

William, son of Samuel and Rachel Callen, bapt. 29 Jun 1800, b. 5 Sep 1799, Northampton.

Samuel, son of Samuel and Margaret Polk, bapt. 30 Aug 1800, b. 27 May 1800, Warminster.

Elizabeth, dau of John and Anne Long, bapt. 25 Oct 1800, b. 18 Aug 1800, Warrington.

James, son of Robert and Mary Forsythe, bapt. 29 Dec 1800, b. 23 Apr 1767, New Britain.

Mary, dau of James and Anne Forsythe, bapt. 29 Dec 1800, b. 5 May 1790, New Britain.

Jane, dau of James and Anne Forsythe, bapt. 29 Dec 1800, b. 19 Jul 1792, New Britain.

Margaret, dau of James and Anne Forsythe, bapt. 29 Dec 1800, b. 28 Apr 1796, New Britain.

Thomas H., son of James and Anne Forsythe, bapt. 29 Dec 1800, b. 22 May 1800, New Britain.

Hugh, son of James and Elizabeth Adams, bapt. 25 Jan 1801, b. 22 Nov 1800, Northampton.

David, son of John and Jane Todd, bapt. 8 Feb 1801, b. [blank], New Britain.

Martha, dau of John and Mary Mann, bapt. 8 Feb 1801, b. 4 Sep 1800, Warwick.

John, son of Thomas and Mary Clemens, bapt. 24 Feb 1801, b. 31 Jul 1800, Horsham.

John, son of John and Martha Harvey, bapt. 25 Mar 1801, b. 24 Dec 1800, Warminster.

Charlotte, dau of Robert and Mary Walker, bapt. 1 May 1801, b. 10 Dec 1799,

Warrington.

Robert H., son of Robert and Mary Walker, bapt. 9 May 1801, b. 17 Feb 1801, Warrington.

Lewis, son of William and Sarah Long, bapt. 9 May 1801, b. 9 Oct 1800, Warrington.

James, son of Robert and Mary Wallace, bapt. 11 May 1801, b. 29 Dec 1800, Warwick.

Elizabeth, dau of Samuel and Rachel Callen, bapt. 30 Jun 1801, b. 30 Jan 1801, Warminster.

Samuel, son of William and Mary McEwen, bapt. 30 Jun 1801, b. 26 Nov 1798, Warwick.

John, son of William and Mary McEwen, bapt. 30 Jun 1801, b. 9 Mar 1801, Warwick.

Henry, son of John and Agnes Kerr, bapt. 28 Jul 1801, b. 27 Nov 1800, Warwick.

Mary, dau of William and Margaret Long, bapt. 13 Aug 1801, b. 24 May 1801, Warrington.

Isabella L., dau of James and Margaret Ray, bapt. 30 Aug 1801, b. 3 Feb 1801, Horsham.

Eliz., dau of Wm and Rebecca Whittenham, bapt. 2 Nov 1801, b. 10 May 1801, Warrington.

Hugh, son of Robert and Frances Mearns, bapt. 1 Jan 1802, b. 2 Nov 1801, Warwick.

Jane, dau of John and Jane Carr, bapt. 18 Jan 1802, b. 21 Jan 1799, Warwick.

Priscilla, dau of John and Jane Carr, bapt. 18 Jan 1802, b. 20 Nov 1800, Warwick.

John, son of Gideon and Elizabeth Prior, bapt. 31 Jan 1802, b. 13 Oct 1801, Warminster.

Joseph, son of John and Mary Rankin, bapt. 21 Mar 1802, b. 20 Dec 1801, Horsham.

Hiram Jones, son of Hannah Jones and [blank], bapt. 6 Jun 1802, b. 24 Feb 1801, Warrington.

John M., son of John and Anna Long, bapt. 6 Nov 1802, b. 6 Feb 1802, Warrington.

Marriages

James Scout, Warminster, Frances Lewis, Warrington, 1 Jun 1788.

Frederick Scholl, New Britain, Catharine Bartleson, Montgomery Twp., 27 Jun 1788.

Robert Miller, Northampton Co, Sarah Simpson, Buckingham, 18 Nov 1788.

Adam Kerr Jr., Warminster, Frances Jamison, Warwick, 16 Apr 1789.

Jesse Barnes, Warminster, Esther Durling, Moreland, 10 Sep 1789.

William Robins, Buckingham, Elizabeth Loughead, Buckingham, 29 Oct 1789.
James Forsythe, New Britain, Anne Kelso, New Britain, 3 Dec 1789.
Amos Childs, Horsham, Jane White, Horsham, 3 Dec 1789.
Joseph Hough, Horsham, Elizabeth Marple, Horsham, 13 Dec 1789.
Peter Jordon, Warrington, Martha Forster, Warrington, 20 Dec 1789.
Levi Brown, Buckingham, Sarah Bennet, Buckingham, 29 Jan 1790.
Adam Stuart, Northampton, Jane Feaster, Northampton, 11 Feb 1790.
Thomas Clemens, Warrington, Mary Quce, Horsham, 23 Feb 1790.
Henry Maskill, Buckingham, Rachel Clossin, Wrightstown, 26 Mar 1790.
Samuel Bye, Solebury, Elizabeth Redding, New Jersey, 12 Aug 1790.
Wm Davis Taylor, Philadelphia, Emma Smith, Philadelphia, Aug 1790.
Joseph Maklim, Hiltown, Agnes Williams, Hiltown, 30 Aug 1790.
Benjamin Worthington, New Britain, Martha Loughead, Buckingham, 30 Nov 1790.
Joseph Whitton, Warminster, Elizabeth Long, Warwick, 9 Dec 1790.
John Hubbs, Moreland (Credo), Susanna Hendricks, Moreland, 14 Jan 1791.
Jacob Vandyke, Northampton, Alice Craven, Warminster, 31 Mar 1791.
William Lukens, Horsham, Mary Nelson, Horsham, 7 Apr 1791.
David Edwards, Abington, Rebekah Walton, Philadelphia, 9 May 1791.
Robert Ditterline, New Britain, Catharine Bergey, New Britain, 7 Jul 1791.
John Otter, Warwick, Sarah Poole, Warwick, 18 Jul 1791.
John Leech, Solebury, Catharine Hagerman, Solebury, 21 Jul 1791.
Jesse Childs, Horsham, Hannah Armitage, Horsham, 6 Sep 1791.
John Connard, Buckingham, Anna Simpson, Buckingham, 8 Sep 1791.
[blank] Cruzen, Northampton, [blank] Cornell, Northampton, 13 Oct 1791.
Thomas Lovett, Warwick, Elizabeth Poole, Warwick, 13 Oct 1791.
Jonathan Rich, Plumstead, Mary Snodgrass, New Britain, 5 Jan 1792.
Enoch Harvey, Warwick, Sarah Stewart, New Britain, 20 Mar 1792.
Hugh McGoochin, Warrington, Mary Davidson, Warrington, 26 Apr 1792.
James McElroy, Nockamixon, Jane Ramsey, Nockamixon, 3 May 1792.
Andrew Long, Warwick, Mary Carr, Warwick, 9 May 1792.
Alexander Carothers, Tinicum, Agnes Dunn, Tinicum, 9 Aug 1792.
William Ramsey, Warwick, Anne Baird, Warwick, 11 Oct 1792.
Robert Wallace, Warwick, Mary Long, Warwick, 23 Nov 1792.
John Kelly, Buckingham, Agnes Clawson, Buckingham, 28 Nov 1792.
John Beans, Warminster, Elizabeth Jenkins, Upper Dublin, 6 Dec 1792.
Andrew Mearns, Cecil Co, MD, Margaret McGraudy, Warwick, 21 Feb 1793.
Joseph Vandevender, Warminster, Mary James, Warminster, 6 Mar 1793.
Septimus Tucker, Warwick, Elizabeth Davis, Solebury, 29 Mar 1793.
Richard Barclay, Warrington, [blank] Smith, Montgomery, 3 Apr 1793.
Edward Malawn, Horsham, Jane Holt, Horsham, 25 Apr 1793.
James Dunlap, Buckingham, Julianna Shewell, New Britain, 16 May 1793.

Thomas Dungan, Germantown, Elizabeth Dungan, Northampton, 19 May 1793.
Benjamin Watson, Lower Makefield, Hannah McKinstry, New Britain, 10 Jun 1793.
William Edwards, Northampton, Agnes Rickey, Warminster, 7 Jul 1793.
Barnard Vanhorn, Warmister, Charity Murray, Warminster, 22 Aug 1793.
Jonathan Walton, Warminster, Agnes Vanpelt, Northhampton, 3 Oct 1793.
John Simpson, Horsham, Rebekah Weir, New Britain, 17 Oct 1793.
William Dungan, New Britain, Alice Morris, Hiltown, 22 Oct 1793.
Charles Vansant, Southampton, Edith Cravan, Warminster, 7 Nov 1793.
James Craig, New Britain, Elizabeth Fulton, New Britain, 28 Nov 1793.
James Sample, Buckingham, Mary Bormer, Buckingham, 9 Dec 1793.
Jacob Sheat, Warrington, Christianna Foster, Warrington, 31 Dec 1793.
Robert Mearns, Warwick, Frances Bogart, Willow Grove, 11 Feb 1794.
John Roney, Jr., Warminster, Mary Young, Warminster, 26 Mar 1794.
Barnard Vanhorn, Upper Makefield, Mary Long, Warrington, 10 Apr 1794.
Jesse Anderson, Warwick, Elizabeth Simpson, Warwick, 15 May 1794.
John Fry, Montgomery, Mary Jones, Tomasin Twp., 3 Jul 1794.
Joseph Wright, Horsham, [blank] Wilson, Montgomery, 4 Sep 1794.
Benjamin Foster, Warrington, Catharine Kinney, Warrington, 11 Sep 1794.
Thomas Dungan, Northampton, Sarah Kruzen, Northampton, 23 Sep 1794.
James Means, Cumberland Co., Margaret Jamison, Warwick, 23 Sep 1794.
Moses Shaw, New Britain, Guzelda Jamison, Warwick, 7 Oct 1794.
William Clauson, Upper Makefield, Sarah Wall, Solebury, 19 Nov 1794.
Robert Walker, Warrington, Mary Hough, Warwick, 27 Nov 1794.
William Kimball, Northampton, Rachel Dungan, Northampton, 4 Dec 1794.
Henry Harding, Northampton, Martha Edwards, Northampton, 18 Dec 1794.
Abner Ely, Solebury, Jane Wiley, Solebury, 1 Jan 1795.
William Yerkes, Moreland, Letitia Esther Long, Warrington, 22 Jan 1795.
John Ratcliff, Warwick, Jane Torrence, Warrington, 12 Feb 1795.
Abraham Lapp, Buckingham, Susanna Bergey, Buckingham, 26 Feb 1795.
Dr. Wm Ramsey, Warwick, Rebekah Simpson, Buckingham, 27 Feb 1795.
Jacob Madeira, Warrington, [blank] Harris, Montgomery, 3 Mar 1795.
Peter Carr, Warminster, Elizabeth Rapp, Warminster, 12 Mar 1795.
James Adams, Northampton, Elizabeth Vansant, Warminster, 26 Mar 1795.
Innis Conard, Buckingham, Sarah Kirk, Wrightstown, 7 Apr 1795.
Philip Foulkrod, Horsham, Elizabeth Cress, Horsham, 18 Jun 1795.
Francis Davidson, Warrington, Mary Carnaghan, Warrington, 30 Jul 1795.
Cornelius Carrell, Warminster, Joice Palmer, Upper Makefield, 3 Sep 1795.
Abraham Guild, Warwick, Mary Gorgas, Warwick, 17 Sep 1795.
John Boyd, Northampton, [blank] McNeil, Moreland, 26 Nov 1795.
Cornelius Vanhorn, Solebury, Mary Bennet, Buckingham, 3 Dec 1795.
Jesse Murdock, Wrightstown, Jane Carr, Horsham, 3 Feb 1796.

Jonathan Delany, Warminster, Anne Sutphen. Warminster, 25 Feb 1796.
Jonathan Smith, Warrington, Anne Simpson, Horsham, 25 Feb 1796.
William Green, New Britain, Tamar Robinson, New Britain, 1 Jan 1796.
Ezekiel Shoemaker, Montgomery, Anne Doyl, Horsham, 24 Mar 1796.
John Torrence, Warrington, Mary Shaw, Warrington, 1 Apr 1796.
John Harvey, Warminster, Martha Henderson, Warminster, (15?) Mar 1796.
William Ingles, Warwick, Mary Cornwall, Kensington, 9 Apr 1796.
William McEwen, Warminster, Mary Hynes, Montgomery, 12 Apr 1796.
Col. James Johnston, Antrim, Franklin Co., Jane Park, Philadelphia, 13 Apr 1796.
Joseph Haire, New Britain, Rebekah Marple, Warwick, 14 Apr 1796.
Eber Gilbert, Warwick, Mary Kelly, Warwick, 23 Apr 1796.
Jesse Paul, Horsham, Elizabeth Collom, Horsham, 30 Jun 1796.
Caleb Perkins, Brandywine Hd., Elizabeth Christine, Horsham, 11 Oct 1796.
[blank] Mackey, Chester Co, Mary Wright, Horsham, 7 Dec 1796.
James Patterson, Warwick, Bretta Simpson, Buckingham, 5 Jan 1797.
James Watson, Warwick, Elizabeth Titus, Warwick, 19 Jan 1797.
John Vandevender, Doylestown, Elizabeth Roney, Warrington, 16 Feb 1797.
George Walters, Warwick, Catharine Walters, Buckingham, 28 Feb 1797.
Cornelius Dungan, Northampton, Agnes Dungan, Northampton, 15 Mar 1797.
Matthew Greer, Plumstead, Sarah Snodgrass, New Britain, 23 Mar 1797.
Henry Harkle, Graeme Park, Mary Connard, Graeme Park, 2 Apr 1797.
Samuel McClean, Horsham, Jane Long, Warwick, 4 May 1797.
[blank] Richards, Philadelphia, Elizabeth Adams, Northampton, 1 Jun 1797.
David Gill, Warrington, Jane Young, Warrington, 21 Jul 1797.
Robert Gross, Warwick, Jane Hoy, Philadelphia, 19 Sep 1797.
Marshal Means, Franklin Co., Mary Jamison, Warwick, 27 Sep 1797.
Thomas Beans, Moreland, Christianna Craven, Warminster, 7 Dec 1797.
James Carrell, Tinicum, Jane Abernathy, Tinicum, 22 Dec 1797.
James Morris, Philadelphia, Jane Thompson, Philadelphia, 9 Jan 1798.
Amos Dungan, Warminster, Eleanor Lukens, Warminster, 2 Feb 1798.
Thomas Percy, Northampton, Charity Dungan, Northampton, 6 Feb 1798.
Daniel Larue, Middletown, Elizabeth Vandegrift, Bensalem, 8 Feb 1798.
John Hibbs, Northampton, Mary Fanning, Northampton, 3 May 1798.
Jacob Heisler, Warminster, Sarah Walton, Warminster, 30 May 1798.
Joseph Cowell, Solebury, Rebecca Morrison, Solebury, 25 Jul 1798.
Silas Barton, Warwick, Hannah Tanner, Amwell, NJ, 18 Sep 1798.
Andrew Reid, Warminster, Elizabeth Vansant, Warminster, 18 Oct 1798.
Joseph McLean, Warminster, Elizabeth Griffith, Warminster, 22 Nov 1798.
John Bryan, Bedminster, Elizabeth Gutcheling, New Britain, 20 Dec 1798.
John Rutherford, Moreland, Mary Gloan, Gloucester Co, NJ, 1 Jan 1799.
Samuel Parker, Warrington, Rebecca McConnel, Warrington, 4 Mar 1799.

William Cannon, Upper Dublin, Elizabeth Warner, Moreland, 4 Apr 1799.
[blank] Cornelle, Northampton, Mary Feaster, Northampton, 30 May 1799.
Samuel McCallen, Warminster, Rachel James, Warminster, 30 May 1799.
Aaron Vansant, Northampton, Margaret Keith, Horsham, 3 Sep 1799.
Elias Larkins, Buckingham, Elizabeth Sebring, Solebury, 3 Oct 1799.
Jacob Rutherford, Moreland, Elizabeth Shelmire, Moreland, 17 Oct 1799.
William Beatty, Columbia, Lancaster Co, Eleanor Polk, Warwick, 8 Nov 1799.
Morgan Meredith, New Britain, Hannah Roberts, Warwick, 26 Dec 1799.
Moses McClean, Horsham, Elizabeth Dougherty, Warwick, 30 Oct 1800.
John Carr, Warminster, Esther Ayres, Moreland, 20 Nov 1800.
Jacob Creer, Moreland, Rachel Fisher, Abington, 20 Nov 1800.
Henry Johnson, Hatfield, Margaret Millar, New Britain, 25 Nov 1800.
John Warner, Moreland, Elizabeth Eldridge, Moreland, 7 Jan 1801.
William Poole, Warwick, Martha Carver, Warwick, 15 Jan 1801.
Andrew McEwen, Warrington, Jane Flack, New Britain, 26 Jan 1801.
William Johnson, Warwick, Britta Barton, Wrightstown, 26 Feb 1801.
Robert Lear, Wrightstown, Mary Meloy, Wrightstown, 26 Feb 1801.
William Long, Warrington, Margaret Bothwell, Warrington, 17 Mar 1801.
Thomas Flack, New Britain, Sarah McEwen, Warrington, 26 Mar 1801.
Isaac Carrell, Warminster, Elizabeth Lefferts, Northampton, 7 May 1801.
Abel Fitzwater, Moreland, Esther Foster, Abington, 24 Dec 1801.
Cornelius Wynkoop, Warminster, Elizabeth Murray, Horsham, 24 Dec 1801.
Archibald Scott, Warwick, Anne Titus, Warwick, 4 Mar 1802.
John Johnson, Abington, Hannah Dubree, Abington, 6 Mar 1802.
Jonathan Livezey, Abington, Elizabeth Dehaven, Northwales, 9 Aug 1802.
Rodman Lovett, Warwick, Elizabeth Roberts, Warwick, 14 Oct 1802.
John Cummings, Philadelphia, Martha Doyle, Warwick, 20 Oct 1802.
[blank] Harrow, New Britain, Anne Snodgrass, New Britain, 9 Dec 1802.
William White, Horsham, Jane Wright, Horsham, 23 Dec 1802.
Jacob Fowler, Hatfield, Barbara Hammer, Warrington, 16 Jan 1803.
Samuel Holme, Horsham, Martha Mann, Horsham, 3 Mar 1803.
Stephen Banes, Warminster, Agnes Ramsey, Warwick, 17 Mar 1803.
James Flack, Buckingham, Rachel Jamison, Warwick, 30 Mar 1803.

THE EVANGELICAL LUTHERAN CONGREGATION AT TINICUM

Baptisms

1760

12 Mar Son of Balthasar Köhler, sponsor, Georg Lang.

Ludwig, son of Leonhard Bock, sponsor, Ludwig Lang.
Johann, s. of Nicolaus Weickert, sponsor Johann Antony.

1761

12 Feb. Johann, s. of Bernhard Sigmann, sponsor, Johann Bissbing.
1 Mar. Catharina d. of Johann Nuss, sponsor Adam Ernst.
13 Apr. Johann Ludwig, s. of Peter Lang, sponsor Ludwig Lang.
Maria, d. of Jacob Fuchs, sponsor Adam Ernst.
11 May. Bernard, s. of Chistoph Sigmann, sponsor Bernhard Sigmann.
Adam, s. of Phillipp Gruber, sponsor Nicolause Gruber.
16 Jun. Johann Jacob, s. of George Fuchs, sponsor Joh. Jacob Fuchs.
Anna Margaretha, d. of Jacob Jerling, sponsor Johann Nicolauss Gruber.
21 Jun. Elisabetha, d. of Heinrich Kopp, sponsor George Fuchs.
15 Aug. David, s. of David Schmidt, sponsor Friedrich Bohner.
Johann Phillipp, s. of Hermann Schumann, sponsor Phillipp Behr.
Georg Ludwig, s. of Michael Wierman, sponsor, Georg Ludwig Lang.
7 Sep. Ester Geist, born Klemmer.
Susanna, d. of Rudolph Drach, sponsor Peter Jung.
8br. Clara Catharina, d. of Georg Mann, sponsor Bernhard Sigmann.
9br. Maria Catharina, d. of Johann Herbst Loehr, sponsor Peter Lauchs.

1762

27 Jan. Johann, s. of Friedrich Bohner, sponsor The Father.
22 Feb. Johann Martin, s. of Johann Thomas, sponsor Johann Martin Frõhlich.
3 Apr. Eva Rosina, d. of Jacob Geist, sponsor himself.
Georg Adam, s. of Adam Ernst, sponsor George Adam Hellepart.
Maria Catharina Elisabeth, d. of George Fuchs.

1760

29 May. Anna Margaretha, d. of Georg Adam Hellepart, sponsors George Gressmann and his wife.

1762

7 May. Johann, s. of George Phillip Lang, sponsor Bernhard Sigmann.
15 Aug. Maria Barbara, d. of Leonhard Bockly, sponsor Phillipp Muth.
Johann Jacob, s. of Johann Strauss, sponsor Jacob Geist.
Johann Heinrich, s. of Nicolaus Gruber, sponsor Hermann Schumann.
14 7br. Rahel, the father Hannes Fricker Muth, sponsors Bernhard Sigmann, Georg Sigmann, Jacob Nuss.
3 8br. Johann Phill, s. of Arnold Schumann, sponsor Phillipp Lehr.
3 grandsons of John Schmidt.

6 9br. Heinrich, s. of Johann Schumann, sponsor himself.
Bernhard, s. of Georg Sigmann, sponsor Bernhard Sigmann.

1763

27 Feb. Anna Margaretha, d. of Jerret Lehr, sponsor Chur. Caspar.
Johann Friedrich, s. of Friedrich Fuchs, sponsor Heinrich Schlatter.
Wilhelm, s. of Nicolauss Weigert, sponsor Balthasar Kõhler.
Anna Maria, d. of Caspar Carl, sponsor Anna Maria Lauch.

14 Apr. Elisabetha, d. of Michael Wiermann, sponsor Hanness Kuster.
Gabriel, s. of Hanness Kuster, sponsor Georg Lang.

24 D. Johann, s. of Georg Adam Hellepart, sponsor Hannes Schnouffer. Date of Birth April 15th.

25 Jun. Maria Catharina, d. of Bernhard Sigmann, sponsor Phillip Lang. Date of Birth 27th May.
Maria Elisabetha, d. of Peter Lang, sponsor Ludwig Lang.
Anna Dorothea, d. of Heinrich Kopp, sponsor Johann Fehr.

24 Jul. Johann, s. of Teobald Fuchs, sponsor, Johann Fuchs.
Johann Georg, s. of Carl Stier, sponsor Bernhard Schneider.
Johann, s. of Wilhelm Albert, sponsor Georg Adam Hellepart.

14 Aug. Maria Magdalena, d. of Hermann Schumann, sponsor Xstian Marburger.

1 Jan. Bernhard Sigmann, sponsor Johann Georg Sigmann. Date of Birth 1752, 10 xbr.

1763 27 Feb. Johann Heinrich, s. of Friedrich Fuchs, sponsor Conrad Reffy.

1756 17 Jul. Joh. Matheis, s. of Matheis Reffi, sponsors Conrad Reffy and Matheis Schlatter.

1763 8 7br. Anna Catharina, d. of Henrich Litsch, sponsors Peter Sein and Johann Fehrs child.

1757 28 xbr. Johann Jacob, s. of Matheis Reffy, sponsor Jacob Lunger.

1759 Anna Clara, d. of Mathaes Reffy, sponsor Matheis Scholotter.

1764 Johann, s. of Teobald Fuchs, sponsor Johann Fuchs.

1764

in Aug. Johann Georg, s. of Carl Stier, sponsor Bernhard Schneider.
in Aug. Johann, s. of William Albert, sponsor Georg Adam Hellepart.

1764 8 Jan. Georg, s. of Thomas Diez, sponsor Georg Sigmann.

1764 Elisabetha Barbara, d. of Jacob Jarling, sponsor himself. Date of Birth 30 xbr 1763.

1764
18 Mar. Henrich, s. of Peter Sayn, sponsor Peter Litsch.
1 Apr. Georg Christian, s. of Gottfrid Bohner, sponsor Georg Sigmann.
23 Apr. Johann Georg, s. of Ludwig Lang, sponsor Georg Lang.
20 May. Anna Elisabetha, d. of Johann Engel, sponsor Fridrich Bohner.
10 Jun. Gottfried, s. of Peter Sein, sponsor Gottfried Bohner.
19 Jun. Johann, s. of Leonhard Geist, sponsor himself.

1764 12 Jun. Johann Georg, s. of Georg Fux, sponsor Nicolaus Fuchs.

1764 22 7br. Elisabesha Catharina, d. of Nicolaus Weigert.

1765 10 Mar. Georg Adam, s. of Georg Adam Hellepart, sponsor Georg Sigmann.

1765 26 Feb. Bernhard, s. of Georg Lang, sponsor Bernhard Sigmann.

1765 30 7br. Ester, d. of Christoph Sigmann. Date of birth Apr 3rd.

1765
9 Apr. Anna Catharina, d. of Michael Wiermann, sponsor Georg Phillip Lang.
8 May. Anna Maria, d. of John Nuss, sponsor Nicolas Wigert.
2 Jun. Johann, s. of John Schumann, sponsor Hermann Schumann.
2 Jun. Johann Siemon, s. of Herman Schumann, sponsor Nicolaus Gruber.

1765 15 7br. Maria Magdalena, d. of Nicolaus Gruber. Date of birth 8 7br.

1761 or 1767 8 Mar. Catharina, d. of John Nuss, sponsors Adam Ernst & his wife.

1767 8 7br. Maria Elisabeth, d. of John Nuss, sponsor Georg Adam Hellepart.

1771
12 May. Georg Adam, s. of Michael Worman, sponsor Georg Adam Hellepart. Date of birth 4 Mar 1771.
2 May. Anna Elisabetha, d. of Theobald Fox, sponsor Georg Adam Hellepart. Date of birth 17 Mar.

1769

1 Jun. Son of Nicolaus Fux, sponsors were Jacob Fux and his wife.
2 Jul. Maria Margaretha, d. of Theobald Fux, sponsor Nicolaus Fux.

<u>1769</u> 17 7br. Elisabetha, d. of Georg Fux, sponsor Theobald Fox and his wife.

<u>1770</u> 10 Jan. [blank] of Johann Carl [blank].

<u>1770</u>
2 7br. Georg Adam, son of Jacob Fuss, witnesses Georg Adam Hellepart and his wife. Date of birth 29 Apr.

<u>1768</u> in 8br. Johann, son of Jacob Nuss, sponsor Johann Nuss.

<u>1771</u>
14 Apr. Johann, s. of Johann Nuss, witnesses Jacob Nuss and his wife. Date of birth 13 Feb.
14 Apr. Maria Catharina, d. of Peter Pissbing, witness [blank]. Date of birth 14 Mar.
14 Apr. Elisabetha, d. of Ludwig Lang, witness, Herman Schuman and wife. Date of birth 29 Mar.
12 May. Johann Georg, s. of Peter Seyn, witness himself.

<u>1771</u> Friedrich, s. of Johann Fley, witness himself.

<u>1771</u>
9 Jun. Catharina Barbara, d. of Andreas Emrich, sponsor Cath. Barb. Weidmayer.
Johann Phillipp, son of Georg Fux, sponsor Michael Wormann.

<u>1772</u>
24 May. Anna Elisabetha, d. of Johann Carl, sponsor Friedrich Kõnig.
Anna Kunigunda, d. of Caspar Carl, sponsor Joh. Jacob Carl.
Anna Margaretha, d. of John Schuman, sponsor Marg. Wild Angerin (Wildanger).
Eva Catharina, d. of Jacob Fehr, sponsor Jacob Geist.
[blank] of Johann Angelmayer, sponsor Caspar Freyling.
Elisabetha, d. of Jacob Nuss, sponsor Georg Fux.
Teobald, s. of Jacob Bergstrasser, sponsor Theobald Fux.

<u>1772</u>
3 7br. Johann Phillip, s. of Nicolaus Straus, sponsor Phillip Herpel.
18 8br. Elisabetha, d. of Matheis Tyson, sponsor Johann Fehr.

1747
4 Mar. Is born to Georg Sigmann a son. Date of birth 4 Mar 1747. Sponsor Christoph Sigmann.
Barbara, sponsor Bernhard Sigman. Date of birth 13 xbr 1748.
Margaretha, d. of Georg Sigman, sponsors Bernhard Heinrich and his wife. Date of birth 28 Feb 1751.
Baltasar, sponsor Balthasar Fuchs. Date of birth 7br 1753.
Georg, sponsor Georg Mann. Date of birth Jun 1756.
Susanna, sponsor Jacob Hasle. Date of birth Jun 1757.
Georg, sponsor Bernhard Sigman, the mother of the child is Barbara. Date of birth 1760.
Bernhard, sponsor Bernhard Sigmann, mother Barbara, born Pissbing. Date of birth 7br 1762.
The father of the above children is Georg Sigmann and his wife Barbara Pissbing.

1764 2 7br. Heinrich, sponsor Gabriel Gamely and Friedrich Bohner.

1764 9 Nov. Maria Magdalena, d. of Peder Jung, sponsor Johanurs Nunamacher.

1788
2 Feb. Johannes, s. of Johannes Schwab, godparents George Kealer and Elizabeth Gruver.
Daniel, s. of Daniel Snyder, sponsor himself.

1788
12 Oct. Anna Maria, d. of Johannes Habacht, sponsor, Killian Kresler.
Elisabeth, d. of Johannes Bergstrasser, sponsor Peter Lang and wife.
Johannes Michael, s. of Joh. Michael Straus, sponsors Johannes Bergstrasser and wife.
Nicolaus, s. of Abraham Yungen, sponsors Nicolaus Weicker and wife. Date of birth 25 Aug 1788.

1753
8 Jan. Johann Georg, s. of Bernhard Sigman, sponsor Georg Sigman. Date of birth 13 xbr 1752.

1754
Aug. Bernhard, sponsor Bernh. Henrich Pisbing. Date of birth Aug 1754.
Willem, sponsor William Fayser. Date of birth 1757.
Johannes, sponsor Joh. Bisbing. Date of birth 12 Feb 1761.

Catharina, sponsors Georg Lang and wife Catharina. Date of birth 27 May 1763.

Bernhard Sigman is the father of these children with his wife Clara, born Pisbing.

8br. Was born at 7 o'clock in the evening a son named Christoph, sponsor Peter Bissbing. Date of birth 20 Aug 1767.

1767 27 Feb. Filib, son of Peder Jung, sponsor Philib Fuchs.

1793

20 May. Johannes, s. of Johannes Fehr, the mother Elisabeth, sponsors Andreas Lauk and Maria Schuhman. Date of birth 7 Jan.

Joseph, father Joseph Lohr? m. Elisabeth, sponsors the parents. Date of birth 21 Mar.

Margaret, f. Peter Lang, Elisabeth, sponsors Phillip Kruger and wife. Date of birth 19 May.

21 Jul. Johannes, f. Henrich Sallate, m. Catherina. Date of birth 28 May.

1794

23 Mar. Henrich, f. Benjamin Sallate, the mother Margareth, sponsors Henrich Sallate and wife.

Cathrina, father Peter Geist, m. Ester, witnesses Friedrich Geist and wife. Date of birth 25 Dec 1793.

Aug. 5. Benjamin, f. Ludwig Sommer, m. Cathrina, witnesses Benjamin Sommer and wife. Date of birth 14 Jul.

1794

3 May. Samuel, father Johannes Bergstrasser, m. Anna, witnesses themselves. Date of birth 28 Feb.

4 May. Johan Jacob and Johan Friedrich. The father Wilhelm Kesler, the m. Anna Maria, witnesses Ludwig Lang and his wife, Georg Most and wife. Date of birth 15 Apr.

10 Aug. Johan Georg, f. Bernhard Nuss, m. Elisabeth, witnesses Georg Nuss and wife. Date of birth 16 Jun.

1759

10 Apr. Georg Adam Hellepart was married to Maria Phillippina Schnauffer and is born 22 Aug 1740, Anna Margaretha, daughter of Georg Adam Hellebart, sponsor Anna Marg. Kresman. Date of birth 29 May 1760.

1763

24 Apr. Johannes, a son, sponsor Johannes Schnauffer. Date of birth 15 Apr 1763.
Georg Adam, a son, sponsor George Sigman. Date of birth 14 Jan 1765.
A daughter died. Date of birth 27 Feb 1762.
Bernhard, a son, sponsor Bernhard Sigmann. Date of birth 9 7br 1766.

<u>1769</u>

27 Aug. Anna Elisabetha, a dau., sponsor Ludwig Lang. Date of birth 4 Aug 1769.

<u>1772</u>

8 Mar. Joh. Heinrich, a son, sponsor Adam Ernst. Date of birth 16 Feb 1772.

<u>1774</u>

9 Oct. Friederich Hellebart, parents Georg Adam Hellebart and Phillipbina, godparents Johannes Nees and his wife. Date of birth 7 Sep 1774.

Names of parents and children who were baptized in this community:

30 Mar 1774. Parents Teobald Fucks & wife Margretha, child Anna Maria, godparents Nicolaus Fucks & Margretha, date of birth 28 8br.

1 May 1773. Parents John Nees & Catharina, child Jacob, godparents Palsar Köhler & Maria Barbara, uxor, date of birth 16 Apr 1773.

15 May 1774. Parents Jacob Nees & his wife Magdlena, child Anna Maria, godparents Maria Barbara Köhler & Peter Lang, date of birth 21 Feb 1774.

9 Oct 1774. Parents Johnnes Schuman & his wife Elizabeth, child John William, godparents John William Köhler & Margretha Lang, date of birth 5 Sep 1774.

12 Feb 1775. Parents Magr.[1] Friederik Miller V.D.M. & Anna Maria, child P. Hennrich, Henrich Rappe V.D.M. & Anna Maria & Mr. Henrich, Rumer & Dorethea, date of birth 6 Feb 1775.

19 Feb 1775. Parents Joseph Yoest & Maria Dorethea, child John Joseph, godparents Joseph Yoest & Catharina Rappe, date of birth 2 Jan 1775.

1 Jan 1775. Parents Michael Sulech & Dorathea, child Michael, godparents Michal Eitel & wife Eva?, date of birth 16 Feb 1775.

19 Nov 1780. Parents Herman Schumann & his wife Gertraut, children John William and John Hercon, godparents John William Köhler, Anna Schumann, Peter Schumann & Barbara Köhler, date of birth 22 Oct

---

[1] Probably intended it to mean Major?

1780.

6 Sep. Parent Peter Wentz, child Henrich, godparent Henrich Krämer, date of birth 14 Apr 1788.

9 Jun. Parents Daniel Shnyder & Elisabeth, child Georg, godparents Georg Shnyder & Anna Margareth, date of birth 1 Feb 1783.

30 Jul. Parents Joh. Wilhelm Kohler & Anna Maria, child Joh. George, godparents the grandparents, date of birth 26 Jul 1783.

30 Jul 1783? Parents Jacob Niess & Magdalena, child Maria Susanna, godparents Balthasar Kohler & his wife, date of birth 13 Nov 1782.

10 Aug. Parents Jacob Jerger & wife, child Jacob, godparents Kilian Kresler & Filabina his wife, date of birth 19 Apr 1783.

10 Aug. Parents Peder Lang & Lisabeth, child Johannes, godparents Johannes Lang & Anna Maria Schumann, date of birth 6 Jul.

7 Mar. Parent Wilhelm Köhler, child Johan Wilhelm, godparent Killian Cressler, date of birth 19 Jan 1790.

7 Mar. Parent Antoni Lier?, child Maria Margreta, godparent Philip Gruger, date of birth 25 Sep 1789.

7 Mar 1790. Parent Icoreh Peck, child Johannes, godparent Johannes [faded], date of birth 29 Oct 1789.

19 Sep. Parent John Schwaab, child Wilhelm, godparent Elias Scholl, date of birth 4 Sep 1790.

19 Sep. Parent John Schwaab, child Icoreh Philip, godparent Henrich Philip Dragen, date of birth 4 Sep 1790.

9 Aug. Parent Friedrich Teiss, child Wilhelm, godparents [blank], date of birth 4 Mar 1791.

7 Feb 1789. Parent Manuwell Sallete, child Daniel, godparents Daniel Sallete & Maria Weicker, date of birth [blank].

21 Mar 1789. Parents Peter Lang & wife Elisabeth, child Maria, godparents Peter Lang & wife Elisabeth, date of birth 13 Dec 1788.

14 Jun 1789. Parents Georg Fogel and wife, child Elisabeth, godparents Nicolas Weicker and wife Susannah, date of birth 20 Feb 1789.

14 Jun 1789. Parents Joseph Liehr and wife Elisabeth, child Elisabeth, godparents Hannes Worman and Elisabeth Lang, date of birth 1789. Parent Jacop VanderBeelt, child Wilhelm, godparents [blank], date of birth 21 Mar 1790.

21 Mar 1790. Parent Icoreh Schneyder, child Johann Icoreh, godparents Jacob Swenk and wife, date of birth Christmas day 1789.

3 May 1789. Parent James deLeine, child Christiana Delena, godparents Icoreh Köhler & Maria Weicker, date of birth 23 Mar 1789.

12 Jul 1791. Parent Johannes Bergstresser, child Anna Maria, godparents [blank], date of birth [blank].

8 Aug. Parent Johannes Lehr, child Maria Magdalena, godparents Peter Laux &

Maria Schuhmann, date of birth 16 Apr.

3 Apr. Parent Peter Lange, child Susanna, godparent Johannes Worman, date of birth 25 Dec 1790.

22 May. Parent Icoreh Adam Hellepart, child Icoreh Adam, godparent Jacop Jerger, date of birth 7 Jan 1791.

22 May. Parent Abraham Yongken, child Abraham, godparent Icoreh Weyker, date of birth 18 Mar 1791.

22 May. Parent Joseph Lehr, child Icoreh, godparent Joseph Lehre, date of birth 15 Apr.

1 Sep 1799. Parents Bernd Hellebard & Regina Barbara, child Friederich, godparents parents, date of birth 27 Jul 1799.

29 Sep 1799. Parents Georg Mast & Maria Magdalena, child Susanna, godparents parents, date of birth 22 Feb 1799.

6 Oct 1799. Parents Jacob Volmar & Catharina, child Rebecca, godparents Abraham Vollmar & Rebecca Gorger, date of birth 3 Aug 1799.

6 Oct 1799. Parents Emanuel Salathe & Eva, child Johannes, godparents Johannes Ritshard & Magdalena his wife, date of birth 14 Aug 1799.

6 Oct 1799. Parents Jacob Buschy & Ballet, child Susanna, godparents parents, date of birth 5 Sep 1799.

28 Nov 1801. Parents Georg Weicker & Maria, child Anna, godparents Jacob Jerger & wife, date of birth 1 Apr 1800.

13 Nov 1802. Parents Wiliam Speer & Susanna, child [blank], godparents parents, date of birth 4 Sep 1800.

<u>1793</u>

15 Dec. Henrich, father Henrich Habach, mother Maria, sponsors Michael Worman & wife. Date of birth 2 Nov.

Samuel, father Johannes Worman, mother Susanna, witnesses Peter Lang & wife Elisabeth. Date of birth 19 Aug.

<u>1794</u>

4 May. Cathrina, father Ott, mother Elisabeth, witnesses parents and Maria Habach. Date of birth 1 Mar.

Margareth, f. Daniel Kiester (Hiester?), m. Elisa. Maria, witness Susanna Worman, 6 year old? Date of birth 24 Mar.

Sara, f. Daniel Kiester (Hiester?), m. Elisa Maria, witnesses parents. Date of birth 14 Sep 1792.

Fronica, f. Daniel Kiester (Hiester?) & his consort, witnesses Michael Worman & consort. Date of birth 23 Jan.

10 Aug. Elisabeth, Elias Scholl, m. Gerthrauch, witness Ludwig Lang. Date of birth 23 Apr.

Sep. Anna, f. Thomas Seyl & wife Anna Maria, witnesses Wilhelm Seim & wife Barbara. Date of birth 10 July.

23 Aug. Peter, f. Christopher Härter, m. Susana, sponsors Nicholas Weicker & wife Susanna. Date of birth 1794.
Baptized by Henrich Schmitt.

1795

22 Feb. Nicolaus, f. Daniel Sulata, m. Maria, sponsors Nicolaus Weickert & wife. Date of birth 7 Sep.
Margareth, f. Johannes Hellbart, m. Maria, sponsors Georg Schneider & wife. Date of birth 4 Oct.
Anthony, f. Friedrich Fley, m. Magdalena, sponsor, Antony Lehr. Date of birth 12 Dec.
Friederich, f. Friederich Helepart, m. Elisabetha, sponsors Friederich Theis & his wife Chatarina. Date of birth 22 May 1794.

18 Jul. Johann Jacob, f. Joh. Jacob Naees, m. Maria, sponsors parents. Date of birth 24 Nov 1794.
Susanna, f. Joseph Lehr, m. Elisabeth, sponsors parents. Date of birth [illegible] May.
Joseph, f. Ludwig Sommer, m. Cathrina, sponsors Phillip Gruber & wife. Date of birth 31 May.
Samuel, f. Nicolaus Geres, m. Susanna, sponsors Henrich Sullata & wife. Date of birth 19 Feb.
Cathrina, f. Johannes Worman, m. Susanna, sponsors Michael Worman & wife. Date of birth 5 Jul.
Jacob, f. John Bissy, m. Eva, sponsor Jacob Bissy. Date of birth 13 Apr.
Barbara, f. Peter Kaub, m. Magdalena, sponsors Caspar Freyling & wife. 3 weeks & 20 days old.

1796

11 Sep. Catharina Fuchs, father Bernhard Fuchs, mother Elisabeth, sponsors Johann Zollner & wife. Date of birth 22 Nov 1795.
Dina Kuser, father Daniel Kusser?, godparents Johann Herbet and Dina Weicker. Date of birth 28 May 1796.
Jacob Vollmer, father Jacob Volmer, godparents Jacob Görger and wife. Date of birth 5 Sep 1796.
Susanna Suss, father Johann Suss, godparents David Schmid & Susanna Keggler. Date of birth 5 Nov 1796.
Eva Keggler, father Johann Keggler, godparents the parents. Date of birth 15 Oct 1795.

Maria Magdalena Scholl, father Elias Scholl, godparents Wilhelm Köhler. Date of birth 17 Jul 1796.
Maria Magdalena Laubenstein, father Peter Laubenstein, mother Eliesabeth Laubenstein, godparents the parents. Date of birth 1 May 1796.

30 Oct. Johann Georg Fuchs, father Johann Jacob Fuchs, godparents 1. Johann Georg Fuchs & 2. Eliesabeth Fuchs. Date of birth 28 Feb 1796.
Eliesabeth Teis, father Peter Teis, godparents Henrich Saletin & wife. Date of birth 28 Jun 1796.

<u>1797</u>

17 Apr. Jacob Mast, father Georg Mast, mother Maria Magdelene, godparents parents. Date of birth 11 Dec 1796.
Sara Hellebardt, father Johann Hellebardt, mother Maria, born Theis, godparents Maria Philippina Grasler. Date of birth 16 Oct 1796.

25 Jun. Johann Lutz, father Johann Lutz, mother Dorothea born Stein, godparents the parents. Date of birth 21 Oct 1796.

20 Aug. Johann Hellenbardt, father Georg Hellenbardt, mother Elisabeth, godparents Killian Greslar and wife. Date of birth 29 Mar 1797.
Peter Fuchs, father Leonard Fuchs, mother Eliesabet, godparents the parents. Date of birth 12 Jun 1797.

31 yd. Anna Maria Koehler, father Wilhelm Koehler, mother Anna Maria, godparents Elias Scholl & wife Gertraud. Date of birth 21 Dec.

<u>1798</u>

25 Mar. Joseph Kruger, father Philip Kruger, mother Maria Margeretha, godfather Nicolaus Kruger. Date of birth 11 Feb 1798.
Sara Loehr, father Arnold Löhr, mother Eliesabet, godparents Philipp Kruger and wife. Date of birth 18 Feb 1798.

6 May. Catharina Schreier, father Adam Schreier, mother Charlotte born Brodin, godparents the parents of the child. Date of birth 8 Feb 1798.

20 May. Johannes Byssi, father Johannes Byssi, mother Eva born Hackman?, godparents Daniel Sallada and wife Maria. Date of birth 10 Mar 1798.

20 Jan 1797, Samuel Schneider, father Georg Schneider, mother Margaretha born Hellebardt, godparents the parents. Date of birth 3 Apr 1798.

<u>1798</u>

1 Jul. Samuel Loehr, father Löhr, mother Eliesabet born Gerris, sponsor the parents. Date of birth 1 Mar 1798.

Eliesabet Sallada, father Henrich Sallada, mother Catharina born Keppert, godparents Henrich Alts & wife Catharina. Date of birth 13 Jan 1798.

15 Jul. Catharina Schmidt, father David Schmidt, mother Susanna born Kögler, godparents Christoph Kögler and wife Eva. Date of birth 9 Jun 1798.

1 Jul. Sara Lang, father Johann Lang, mother Maria born Mershal, godmother Eliesabet widow Lang. Date of birth 31 Jan 1798.

26 Aug. Georg Adam Hellebardt, father Johann Hellebardt, mother Maria born Theis, godparents the parents. Date of birth 7 Jul 1797.

9 Sep. Eliesabet Habbach, father Cornelius Habbach, mother Reginna born Schell, godparents Kilian Gresler & wife Philipina? Date of birth 23 Apr 1798.

1799

27 Jul. Joseph Weissel, father Georg Weissel, mother Elisabeth. Date of birth 24 Apr.

Rebecca Lange, father Joseph Lange, the mother Maria, godparents Leonhard Scholl & Elisabeth Sommer, both single. Date of birth 24 Mar.

Johannes Lehr, father Antony Lehr, the mother Clara, godparents Johannes Herbst and Magdalena Lange, both single. Date of birth 17 Feb.

27 Jul. Wilhelm Fuchs, father Bernhard Fuchs, mother Elisabeth, godparents Willhelm Spier & Susanna. Date of birth 4 Jan.

Catharina, illegitimate dau of Solomon Diemer and Elisabeth Leipgab, godparents Jacob Leipgeb & wife Elisabeth

1800

13 Jul. Marereta, parents Henrich Solida & wife Catarina, witnesses parents. Date of birth 22 Mar 1800.

Joseph, parents Peter Shuhman & wife Elisabeth, witnesses Philip Gruber & wife Marceta. Date of birth 18 Jun 1800.

SOUTHAMPTON BAPTIST CHURCH RECORDS

Jenkin Jones, an ordained Elder, came here [from the Welch Tract] with his family about Oct 1726.

1745. The number of members being increased about Southampton, they began to be desirous to be separated from the church to which they did belong; and to be constituted a church distinct from them: which they made known to the Church at Lower Dublin, alias Pennepack.

Petitioners: signed 16 Feb 1745/6. Rachel Dungan, Susannah Thomas, Elizabeth Baldwin, Elizabeth Kellings, Rebeckah Humphrys, Mary Newman, Ann Potts, Sarah Stephens, Elizabeth Morford, Mary Parry, a negro, Sarah Hufty, Lucy Chamberlain, Joanna Gilbert, Eleanor Hart, Elizabeth Yerkes, Elizabeth Gilbert, Elizabeth Watts, Sarah Shaw, Mary Dungan, Grace Morgan, Sarah Murray, Esther Banes, Mary Jones, Mary Gilbert, Elizabeth Hart, Jane Yerkes, John Jones, Clement Dungan, David Dungan, James Dungan, David Rees, Joseph Banes, John Baldwin, John Gilbert, Joseph Hart, Lewis Rees, Isaac Eaton, Silas Yerkes, Oliver Hart, John Hellings, Thomas Dungan, Jeremiah Dungan, Thomas Potts, Nicholas Gilbert, Robert Parsons, Samuel Gilbert, John Hart, Thomas Dungan Junr., Stephen Watts, Joshua Potts, Randal Morgan, John Eaton, John Morford, John Harrison, John Shaw. The Church granted same on 5 April 1746.

16 Aug 1746. John Baldwin and Sarah Stephens were admitted members.
17 Aug Rachel Dungan received.
19 Sep Mary Parry, a Negro received.
18 Oct John Eaton suspended for some unbecoming carriage at the election at Newtown.
20 June 1747. Esther Dungan received a member by letter from the church at Montgomery. Also Martha Eaton, member at New Brittain by her husband John Eaton, a member.

20 May 1749. A report brought against John Baldwin for excess in Drinking and against his wife Elizabeth for another matter. [nothing proved against her]
John Morford and Margaret Fraiser having contracted marriage and proceeded so far as to be published without acquainting the Church now taken notice of. Some were for pardoning them and some condemned them.

17 June. Reference to Samuel Guy and his wife Rebecah; John Hart and his wife Eleanor.

15 July 1749. Joseph Banes excommunicated.
John Morford and his wife Margaret - their business mentioned.
John Baldwin being removed into Moore Land, not much farther from Lower Dublin Meeting House, than from the Southampton, his wife Elizabeth

was desirous to move her membership there, because her father and her sister were members there; letter of dismission granted.

17 Dec 1749 John Morford reported that he had been with Susannah Thomas, as he was appointed, and that she told him, she was confined at home by reason of her husband's mother who lived with them, who being not only old and sickly, but also humoursome and weak in her senses; she could not well be from her.

James Dungan requested a letter of dismission to the church at Lower Dublin, granted.

20 April 1754. Mary Griffith, formerly Mary Coffing, being in the course of Providence, removed far from us, and settled near the Church at Montgomery, desired a letter of dismission which was granted.

21 April 1754. A scandalous report of Hannah Brooks, being too familiar with John Burns.

15 June 1754. Hannah Brooks, re-admitted.

14 Dec 1754, Hannah Brooks informed the Church that she was intended to marry with John Burns and requested their advice and consent but as he was accounted a man of vicious life, she was advised to the contrary.

15 Feb 1755. Since the last meeting Hannah Brooks has married to the said John Burns. She was suspended.

19 April 1755. A report that Samuel Guy and his wife Rebekah (in contempt of law) had used both Sheriff, and his Deputy... ???

19 July 1755. Hannah Burns excommunicated for fornication, proved by her having a child in about 4 months after her marriage.

Sarah Dungan, late Sarah Haffty suspended for marrying without first advising with the Church.

20 Sep Sarah Dungan readmitted.

16 Oct 1756. Mary ---, formerly Newman, went from here with her husband, Jonathan Newman, to Virginia, without any letter of dismission, there being no settled church in the parts where he took her. However there is now a church being settled near where she lives, she by the name of Mary her husband Newman being dead, sent by her brother in law, Samuel Newman to request a letter of dismission from us which was granted.

18 Nov 1758. Hannah Burns readmitted.

16 Dec 1758. Randal Morgan having married a woman of a bad character, he is debarred from serving any more as deacon.

17 Feb 1759. Complaint against Ester Dungan for excess in drinking. She gives reason of infirmities; says she is in need of strong liquor. Suspended.

Died Rev. Joshua Potts, who walked 5 miles to meeting, not being able to bear the motion of a horse and carriage.

16 Jan 1762. Informed that Mary Craven, widow of Peter Craven, was left with 3 small children and is hard set to provide for herself and family.

Joseph Dungan baptized.

20 Feb 1762. William Murry have left money in his will for the purpose of repairing the graveyard.

16 April 1762. Conrad Smith excommunicated.

15 May 1762. Rebecka Yerkas, wife of Stephen Yerkas and Martha Brooks, wife of John Brooks baptized.

14 June 1762. Mr. Davis to visit the Church in Great Valey, of which he is still a member.

14 Aug 1762. John Brooks and Sarah Shaw, wife of Joseph Shaw baptized.

Informed that Thomas Beans had said Mr. Davis was a fornicator, and that Stephen Watts had been drunk, stripd himself naked and run after him half a mile in that condition. He [Thomas Beans] is to clear himself or be excommunicated.

19 Sep 1762. Thomas Beans unable to support his charges, excommunicated.

7 May 1763. Jane Beans requested a letter of dismission to Penepack; this was objected to, and she laid under suspension for her disorderly absenting herself from the Church.

Mary Davis has neglected her place in the Church.

24 Sep 1763. A difference exists between Wm. Folwell and Silas Yerkas.

Elianer Beans, Susannah Rush and Christiana Johnson baptized.

14 Jan 1764. Elizabeth Parsons wife of Robert Parsons and Rachel Prichard, widow, to be baptized.

6 May 1764. David Marpole and his wife Elizabeth baptized.

Grace Webster formerly belonging to the Seventh Day Baptists was admitted a member.

30 June 1764. Elizabeth Sands baptized.

1 Sep 1765. Rebecka Cunningham, wife of Thos. Cunningham, baptized.

9 Nov 1765. Thomas Folwell having lately given evidence in an action wherein his father Wm. Folwell was plaintiff agnst. Silas Yerkas, deft. which by some was judged false or equivocal at least; moved to have him suspended.

It was agreed to give Mary Craven 4 pounds to pay the doctor of setting her son' thighs.

5 July 1766. Sarah Banes, wife of Matthew Banes baptized.

6 Sep 1766. Mary Dungan, wife of Jeremiah Dungan Junr. and Elisabeth Mahlane baptized.

8 Nov 1766. Jeremiah Dungan, son of Clemond Dungal baptized next day.

7 July 1767.A difference has arisen between Rev. Samuel Jones and Joseph Richardson concerning the sale of a Negro woman.

21 May 1768. John Morford and his wife Margaret having for a long time neglected their place in the Church; also he has raised sundry false and scandalous reports against Rev. Samuel Jones.

2 July 1768. A difference has arisen between Jeremiah Dungan and Joseph Richardson about some sheep.

3 Sep 1768. John Morford and his wife excommunicated.

Mr. Jones complains that Joseph Richardson sold him a Negro wench which he said was good and sound and that he knew at the time she was not sound.

6 May 1769. Joseph Richardson excommunicated.

July 1769. Martha Fereby baptized.

14 Feb 1771. Richard Clayton by his last will and testament devised a small sum to the meeting.

21 March 1771. Members to go to David Griffiths and see if he can be got off the Plantation.

4 Jan 1772. Mary Dungan, dau. of Jeremiah Dungan being pregnant and some reports being spread about to the disadvantage of the charactor of Jame Dungan, concerning his correspondence with her: wherefore it is ordered that ... inspect into the matter.

Thomas Folwell readmitted.

The church agrees to abate the rent of David Griffith.

2 May 1772. Abel Morgan being removed to Penepack, desires a letter of dismission.

30 May 1772. Lucretia Cooper baptized.

1 Aug 1772. Isaac Hough and his wife Edith baptized.

13 Aug 1772. Elizabeth Beans, wife of John Beans and dau. of John Shaw; and Mary Clayton, widow and relict of Richard Clayton, dec'd., to be baptized.

10 Sep 1772. Stephen Yerkas and Pheby Marpole to be baptized.

Elias Dungan and Amy Megee to be baptized.

25 Oct 1772. Martha Brooks, dau. of Thomas Brooks and Stephen Yerkas, Elias Dungan, Eme Megee and Pheby Marpole baptized.

1 Nov 1772. Jane Gilbert, dau. of John Gilbert baptized.

12 Dec 1772. Andrew Wiley replaces John Brooks as sexton and in the cleaning of the house.

7 Aug 1773. Harry, Negro slave of Clemond Dungan, baptized.

9 Oct 1773. Elias Yerkas and his wife Rebecka, and James Bray, to baptized tomorrow morning.

11 Dec 1773. Negro Daph, a female slave to Mr. Arthur Watts, baptized.

3 April 1774. James Bray charged with cutting a man's coat, taking and killing a turkey belonging to Francis Jordon; says he is innocent.

12 May 1774. Clemond Dungan alledged that at the last meeting Martha Brooks had asserted several falsehoods concerning her dau. - Yost Venander, Mary Dungan and others, and that Venander wd. prove it. John Brooks then sent for his dau. to support what his wife had said - who affirmed that James, Mary and Ann Dungan, Yost Venander, herself and another young woman, went from a carding match at young Jeremiah Dungans, to his fathers, that it was late in the night when they got there, - that she and the last mentioned young woman went to bed together, and that the next morning she heard the other four persons say amongst themselves that they all slept together, and that James Dungan had procured a petticoat for one of the girls to sleep in. Yost Venander was then heard in support of the charge against Martha Brooks, who says he does not remember going to Clemond Dungans that evening and thinks that Mary Dungan and Sarah Brooks went with him to Old Jeremiah Dungans and that from thence he and Richard Manly went to Cornelius Corsons that same night. James Dungan then complaining that his reputation suffered by the false suggestions of the sd. Martha Brooks, and that the same thing had already been heard and determined by the Church. John Brooks informed that one Mary Megraw had informed him that James Dungan kept company with sd. Mary Dungan in a very disreputable &c. To be investigated.

James Bray excommunicated.

2 Aug 1774. Mary Megraw denies having told John Brooks those things he had asserted.

Clemond Dungan and his sons Jeremiah and James complained of great partiality in the Chruch at the last Quarterly Meeting; insisted upon having Martha Brooks suspended. It was determined that the faults were reciprocal.

14 Aug 1774. Eliner Craven wife of Thomas Craven and dau. of Isaac Hough baptized.

7 Oct 1774. Dr. Toomb's Negro woman baptized.

1 April 1775. Elizabeth Parsons was dissatisfied about her pew the last year; that she did not think it right she should pay for the whole pew.

22 March 1778. Concluded from the present difficulty and danger of our circumstances by reason of our vicinity to the Enemy and the consideration above mentioned to have a vacancy till the first of May next.

The American Army moving on the 19th of June 1778 to the Eastward Mr. Van Horn Preached two Lords days in June and went on to join the Troops. Were vacant a few days excepted till December when Mr. Van Horn returned.

13 Feb 1779. Mr. Vanhorn represented the distress our sister Elizabeth Banes had met with by the mal-conduct of Capt. Pugh and his company of Militia of this county on the night of --- in plundering her house of all her most valuable cloathing and effects. It was moved that a subscription be set on foot for her relief which was agreed to.

1 Jan 1780. Martha Brooks has requested a letter of recommendation through a letter to her sister Hannah Burns which was read; but as the said Martha Brooks was suspended sometime agoe and no concessions accompanying said request, it was resolved that the request cannot be granted.

11 June 1780. Sarah Pritchard baptized.

3 July 1780. Clemond Dungan being called upon answered in justification of absenting himself from our meeting said he had been ill used by the Church --- that they had endeavored to prove his son the father of a bastard child &c.

Jeremiah Dungan appearing and also charging several Brethren with personal private offences.
Mary Richardson likewise being present renders for the reason of her neglecting the assemblies of the Church the dealing of the Church with her husband in his excommunication which she alleged was unjust, &c.
James Dungan suspended.

16 April 1781. Reports are prevailing of Brother Thomas Folwell's frequenting places of horse racing.
17 June 1781. Hannah Yerkes wife of Silas Yerkes was baptized at their own house by Mr. Hughs of Maryland on 15 June.
1 Jan 1783. Isaac Hough Junr received as a member.
11 Oct 1783. Dissatisfaction of some members of the Church with the marriage and conduct of Lucretia Kerril (late Cooper). Edith Hough and Mary Yerkes to enquire and report at our next meeting.

1 Jan 1784. Lucretia Kerril acknowledges that she had been guilty of fornication and that her child was born within seven months and two weeks of her marriage and professed sorrow therefor. Hannah Burns and Martha Dnal cited to appear to declare what knowledge they had of the conduct of Lucretia Kerril.
12 June 1784. Isaac Hough Junr having requested a letter of dismission to the Church at Pennypack, it was approved.
3 Jan 1785. Negro Harry acknowledges drunkenness but promises reformation and is sorry for his conduct.
13 Aug 1785. Brother Anthony Yerkes to give his sister in law the sd. Rebeckah Yerkes notice to attend our next meeting to answer a complaint.
17 June 1786. Letter received from Pennypack Meeting [?] for Rev. and Esteemed brother David Jones.

7 April 1788. Appointed brother William Watts clerk of the Church in the room of Joseph Hart, esq., dec'd.
In the previous period William Watts, Peter Sowerman and Evan Banes were baptized.

11 Oct 1788. Rebekah Yerkes and Elizabeth Colbert baptized.
10 Oct 1789. Elenor Jones and Benjamin Bennet baptized.
4 Jan 1790. Sister Hannah McNeal to be entitled to certain privileges in the old meeting house for one year.

18 June 1790. Negro Harry suspended, lately guilty of drinking to excess and unbecoming behaviour.

Josiah Hart entered a complaint aginst Peter Sowerman for defamation, charging him with having taken a false oath concerning a settlement between them.

9 April 1791. Elenor Marpole baptized.
11 June 1791. John Morford and his wife Margaret having been in a excommunicated state for many years, presented a written acknowledgment of their faults and prayed to be restored to membership. Granted. They also desired a letter of dismission to the Church at New Mitts to which they were more conveniently situated; also granted.
13 Aug 1791. Able Marple, Timothy McGinnes and his wife baptized.
2 Jan 1792. Mr. Jones proposes that he be removed as soon as convenient as he apprehended that his stay among the people could not be conducive either to his or their happiness.
1 Jan 1794. Negro Harry excommunicated.
7 June 1794. Nancy Taylor and Martha Deleny baptized.
7 July 1794. Brother John Shellingsburgh is in needy circumstances and requires assistance.
9 Aug 1794. John Hough and his wife Charity, Betsey Thomas, and Ann Hart wife of Collonel Joseph Hart, Hannah Taylor and Hannah Yerkes baptized.
11 Oct 1794. John Dungan, Ann Hart wife of Josiah Hart and Betsey Hart their dau., Elenor and Mary Hart daus. of Silas Hart and Polly Folwell baptized.
13 Dec 1794. Hannah Hough wife of Thos. Hough, Jane Dungan and Abigal Curtis baptized.
7 Feb 1795. Margery Sowerman, Susan Yerkes and Phee Banes baptized.
11 April 1795. Mrs. Elizabeth and Nathen Marple, Polly Banes, Josiah Banes, Flora (wife of Harry) and James her son Yaff, held as a slave by Thomas Craven but the Lord's freeman, baptized.
10 May 1795. The case of Rebecka Watson dau. of Stephen and Rebecka Yerkes supposedly guilty of incontinency. Found guilty by the appointed committee; suspended.
13 June 1795. Jacob Vanhorn, Rebecka Wood, Susanna Hunter, and Sarah wife of James, baptized.
8 Aug 1795. Peggy Banes and Sally Yerkes baptized.

Southampton Baptist Church - Marriages

Oliver Hart and Sarah Brees were married 23 Feb 1747/8 by Peter Peterson Vanhorn, she being not a member. She was the dau of Henry Brees late of Bensalem decd.

John Morford and Margarett Frazer (eldest dau of Andrew Frazer late of Warminster decd) were married by our minister Joshua Potts 23 May 1749.

Hannah Watts (dau of Stephen Watts) was married to James Smith of Phila by our minister Joshua Potts 14 Jun 1750. She being no member.

Mary Coffing (dau of William Coffing of Horsham) was married to Joseph Griffith (son of Benj Griffith pastor of the Church at Montgomery) 22 Jan 1754. She being no member.

Hannah Brooks (dau of John Brooks late of Southampton decd) was married to John Burns (alias Burnet) – Feb 1755. She being no member.

Mary Oliver was married to Peter Craven by our minister Joshua Potts 7 Jan 1756. He being no member.

Randal Morgan was married to Martha Wilson by our minister Joshua Potts 29 Nov 1758. She being no member.

Isaac Eaton was married to Rebecca Stout by our minister Joshua Potts. She being a member of the Church at Hopewell and dau of David Stout of same place.

Silas Yerkas was married to Hannah Dungan (dau of Thomas Dungan of Warminster) by our minister Joshua Potts 14 Jun 1750. She being no member.

Silas Hart of Warminster Township, Bucks Co was married to Mary Donel of Lower Dublin Township in Phila Co by the Revd Peter Peterson Van Horn 29 Jan 1769 per licence.

Malakiah Richardson and Sarah Dungan both of Northampton Township, Bucks Co married 17 Dec 1773 by the Revd William Van Horn per licence.

Jephany Lott and Alice Vanpelt both of Northampton Township, Bucks Co married 21 Jan 1773 per licence by the Revd William Van Horn.

Benjamin Jones and Susannah Hough both of Warmister Township, Bucks Co were married 17 Jun 1773 per publishment by the Revd William Van Horn.

John Fenton and Sarah Cawley both of Northampton Township, Bucks Co were married per licence by the Revd William Van Horn 20 Jun 1773.

Cornelius Daily and Elizabeth Crewson were married 27 Jun 1773 per licence by the Revd William Vanhorn.

Gabiel Vansant & Joice Bretsford were married 7 Jul 1773 per licence by the Revd William Vanhorn.

Charles Holmes and Mary Corson were married 27 Aug 1773 per licence by the Revd William Vanhorn.

William Bateman and Margeret Porter were married 22 Sep 1773 per licence by the Revd William VanHorn, they were both of Northampton Township, Bucks Co.

John Vanpelt and Susannah Dungan both of Northampton Township, Bucks Co were married 29 Sep 1773 per publishment by the Revd William Van Horn.

Adrian Wynekoop and Sarah Randal both of Northampton Township, Bucks Co were married 4 Nov 1773 per licence by the Revd William Van Horn.

Benjamin Marpole of the Mannor of Moreland, Phila Co and Hannah Dungan of Warwick Township, Bucks Co were married 14 Nov 1773 per licence by the Revd William Van Horn.

William Rees and Susannah Acord were married 20 Jan 1774 per publishment by the Revd William Van Horn.

Abraham Lott and Elizabeth Perry were married per publishment 27 Jan 1774 by the Revd William Van Horn.

John Hough and Charity Venderen both of Warmister Township, Bucks Co were married 19 May 1774 per licence by the Revd William Van Horn.

Abraham Brittan and Keziah Vansant both of Bucks Co were married 21 Sep 1773 by the Revd John Blackwell by licence.

Harman Yerkas of Warminster Township and Mary Clayson of Newbritton Township both in Bucks Co were married 30 Sep 1773 by the Revd Jno Blackwell by licence.

Thomas Bower and Sarah Yerkas both of the Mannor of Moreland, Phila Co were married by the Revd John Blackwell – May 1774 by licence.

Even Johnston and Liddy Groom both of Bucks Co were married in 1774 by the Revd John Blackwell per licence.

George Randal and Sarah Brooks both of Bucks Co were married – Jul 1774 by the Revd John Blackwell per licence.

Josiah Hart (son of Joseph Hart of Warminster, Bucks Co esqr) was married to Mrs. Nancy Watts (dau of Mr. Arthur Watts of Southampton & Co afsd) 11 Jan 1776 by the Revd John Blackwell after being published three Sabbaths at Southampton meeting.

The above register by Joseph Hart esqr.

Henry Courson and Margaret Cornel both of Southampton were married 23 Apr 1775 per licence by Revd William Van Horne.

Benjamin Boutcher and Lydia Benner were married 21 Feb 1776 per licence by Revd William Van Horne.

Amos Dilworth & Hannah Taylor were married 28 Mar 1776 per licence by Revd William Van Horne.

William Carver & Martha Harding were married 11 Apr 1776 per licence by Revd William Van Horne.

Jonathan Budd and Ann Sexton were married 22 Oct 1777 per licence by Revd William Van Horne.

John Morris esqr and Mary Memminger were married May 1777 by Revd William Van Horne.

George Kimble Methodist Preacher & Ann Budd were married 16 Feb 1779 by Revd William Van Horne.

Daniel Coursen & Prudence Carter were married 22 Jan 1780 per licence by Revd William Van Horne.

Stephen Burrows & Elizabeth Watkins were joined together in matrimony 30 Mar 1780 per licence by Revd William Van Horne.

Gilliam Cornel and Jane Cornel were married 11 Jul 1780 per licence by Revd William Van Horne.

Enoch Addis and Nessenger were married 22 Jul 1780 per licence by Revd William Van Horne.

Henry Stoneman & Rachel Fisher were married 21 Sep 1780 per licence by Revd William Van Horne.

Elbert Diew Mont & Catharine Hogeland were married 1 Nov 1780 per licence by Revd William Van Horne.

Godfrey Van Deren & Alice Evans were married 23 Nov 1780 per licence by Revd William Van Horne.

David Dungan Senr & Mary Jones were married 28 Dec 1780 per licence by Revd William Van Horne.

Isaac Hough Junr & Elizabeth Houghton were married 26 Apr 1781 per publishment by Revd William Van Horne.

David Marple & Hannah Maulsbey were married 2 May 1781 per licence by Revd William Van Horne.

John Addis and Mary Strickland were married 17 May 1781 per licence per William Van Horne.

John Bennet and Sarah Van Pelt were married 25 May 1781 per licence by Revd William Van Horne.

Joseph Budd and Mary Fox of NJ were married 25 Oct 1781 per licence by Revd William Van Horne.

Joseph Tomkins & Sarah Dungan were married 2 Nov 1781 per licence by Revd William Van Horne.

Eli Morgan and Elizabeth Yerkes were married 17 Feb 1782 per licence by Revd William Van Horne.

Josiah Matlack and Mary Van Sciver were married 12 Mar 1782 per publishment by Revd William Van Horne.

Alexander Bartley and Mary Shearman were married 28 Mar 1782 per publishment by Revd William Van Horne.

Reading Howel and Catharine Yerkes were married 28 Mar 1782 per publishment by Revd William Van Horne.

George Willard and Jane Kroesen were married 13 Jun 1782 per licence by Revd William Van Horne.

Jacob Johnson and Rachel Sands were married 15 Aug 1782 per [blank] by Revd William Van Horne.

Jacob Johnson and Rachel Sands were married 15 Aug 1782 per [blank] by Revd William Van Horne.

Joshua Breysford and Ann Davis were married 26 Sep 1782 per [blank] by Revd William Van Horne.

Benjamin Jolly and Sarah Jaquess were married 1 Nov 1782 by Revd William Van Horne.

James Vansant & Martha Van Horne were married 17 Dec 1782 per publishment by Revd William Van Horne.

Richard Duffield & Elizabeth Addis were married 9 Feb 1783 per licence by Revd William Van Horne.

Jacob Scott and Esther Vansant were married 17 Mar 1783 per publishment by Revd William Van Horne.

Joseph Carver and Mary Van Sant were married 23 Mar 1783 per licence by Revd William Van Horne.

Thomas Bower and Rachel Fisher were married 27 Mar 1783 per publishment by Revd William Van Horne.

Nathan Comly and Sarah Kirk were married 28 Mar 1783 per licence by Revd William Van Horne.

Abraham Randall and Margaret Swinney were married 19 Jun 1783 per publishment by Revd William Van Horne.

Jacob Pain and Rachel Feaster were married 14 Jul 1783 per publishment by Revd William Van Horne.

George Van Ander & Mary Vandegrift were married 25 Sep 1783 per publishment by Revd William Van Horne.

David Forst esqr & Hannah Harkison were married 29 Sep 1783 per licence by Revd William Van Horne.

Jesse Willard and Esther Duffield were married 2 Oct 1783 per licence by Revd William Van Horne.

John Irwin and Sarah Johnson were married 23 Nov 1783 per publishment by Revd William Van Horne.

Laurance Johnson & Hannah Jackson were married 25 Nov 1783 per publishment by Revd William Van Horne.

Josiah Yerkes Junr & Rachel Edwards were married 2 Dec 1783 per publishment by Revd William Van Horne.

George Kelly and Temperance Blackford were married 3 Dec 1783 per licence by Revd William Van Horne.

Joseph Leedom & Euphame Banes were married 22 Dec 1783 per licence by Revd William Van Horne.

James Jerkes and Rachel Shaw were married 23 Dec 1783 per licence by Revd William Van Horne.

Joseph Hart Junr & Nancy Folwell were married 25 Dec 1783 per publishment by Revd William Van Horne.

Charles Biles & Rachel Leedom were married 31 Dec 1783 per licence by Revd William Van Horne.

John Roberts and Brache Cornel were married 22 Jan 1784 per licence by Revd William Van Horne.

Jesse Dungan and Sarah Comfort were married 5 Feb 1784 per licence by Revd William Van Horne.

Isaac Worthington & Mary Coles were married 2 Mar 1784 per [blank] by Revd William Van Horne.

Lambert Van Dyke & Sophia Van Horne were married 7 Mar 1784 per publishment by Revd William Van Horne.

Timothy McGinnes & Sarah Van Horne were married 10 Mar 1784 per publishment by Revd William Van Horne.

Jacob McVeagh & Amy Marple were married 17 Mar 1784 per licence by Revd William Van Horne.

Jonathan White and Jane Hufty were married 2 Apr 1784 per publishment by Revd William Van Horne.

Isaac Osmond and Rachel States were married 8 Apr 1784 per publishment by Revd William Van Horne.

Benjamin Jones & Sarah Loofbourson were married 22 Apr 1784 per publishment by Revd William Van Horne.

Stephen Burrows and Mary Dickenson were married 31 May 1784 by Revd William Van Horne.

William Wetherill and Rebecka Sacket were married 13 Jul 1784 per licence by Revd William Van Horne.

Richard Venemon and Mary Sheppard were married 28 Nov 1784 per publishment by Revd William Van Horne at Dividing Creek, NJ.

Derick Kroesen and Elizabeth Van Sant were married 6 Jan 1785 per licence by Revd William Van Horne.

John Fisher and Elizabeth States were married 17 Feb 1785 per publishment by Revd William Van Horne.

David Dungan Junr & Sarah Van Horne were married 17 Feb 1785 per publishment by Revd William Van Horne.

Cornelius Cornel and Phebe Cornel were married 24 Mar 1785 per licence by Revd William Van Horne.

John Shellingsburgh & Martha Donal were married 24 Mar 1785 per publishment by Revd William Van Horne.

David Praul and Judith Parry were married 5 Apr 1785 per licence by Revd William Van Horne.

Daniel Runyan and [blank] Morris (Scotts Plains) were married 18 Apr 1785 per licence by revd William Van Horne.

Jacob Pennington & Catharine Van Pelt were married 6 Aug 1785 by Revd William Van Horne.

Joseph Young and Ann Titus were married 9 Nov 1785 per licence by Revd William Van Horne.

John Feaster and Lenah Swenney were married 8 Dec 1785 per licence by Revd William Van Horne.

William Bennet and Catherine Cornell were married 23 Jan 1786 per licence by Revd William Van Horne.

William Watts and Elizabeth Taylor were married 12 Apr 1787 per Runy Runyan.

William Bullis and Anne Taylor were married -- Apr 1793 by Thomas Memminger.

Jacob Yerkes and Sarah Fleming were married -- May 1793 by Thomas Memminger.

Births

Sarah Murray, dau of William Murray of Moor Land and Sarah his wife, was born about 6:00 in the morning 6 Nov 1732 in Moor Land.

Hannah Murray, dau of the said William Murray and Sarah his wife, was born in Moor Land about 6:00 in the morning 6 May 1734.

William Murray, son of the said William Murray and Sarah his wife, was born in Moor Land about 3:00 in the afternoon 4 Jun 1736.

Ruth Murray, dau of the said William Murray and Sarah his wife, was born in Moor Land about 4:00 in the afternoon 3 Apr 1740.

Andrew Murray, son of the said William Murray and Sarah his wife, was born in Moor Land about 8:00 at night 14 Dec 1745.

John Jones, the son of John Jones (now of Moor Land) and Elizabeth his wife (decd) was born about 10:00 in the forenoon 29 Aug 1728 being Thursday in Southampton, Bucks Co.

Mary Jones, dau of the said John Jones and Elizabeth his wife was born 3 May 1730 about 10:00 in the forenoon, being Sunday in Warminster.

Jonathan Jones, son of John Jones and Mary his new wife, was born 10 Jan 1737/8 in More Land.

Joshua Jones, son of the said John Jones and May his wife, was born 9 Mar 1739/40 in the forenoon in Moor Land being Sunday.

Jacob Jones, son of the said John Jones and Mary his wife, was born 24 Mar 1741/2 in Moor Land.

Sarah Jones, dau of the said John Jones and Mary his wife was born 16 Mar 1743/4 before Day being Friday in Moor Land.

Alice Jones, dau of John Jones of Moor Land and Mary his wife, was born 8 Mar 1744/5 about 6:00 in the afternoon in Moorland.

William Hart, son of Joseph Hart of Warminster and Elizabeth his wife, was born about 10:00 at night 4 Dec 1741 being Friday in Warminster. He died 15 Oct 1760 and was buried the next day at Southampton.

John Hart, son of Joseph Hart of Warminster and Elizabeth his wife, was born 29 Nov 1743 about 7:00 in the morning being Tuesday in Warminster.

Silas Hart, son of Joseph Hart of Warminster and Elizabeth his wife, was born 4 Oct 1747 about noon being Sunday in Warminster.

Seth Hart, son of Oliver Hart of Warminster and Sarah his wife, was born near 8:00 in the morning 18 Nov 1748 being Friday in Warminster. He died in Charles Town, SC 22 Sep 1750.

Benjamin Jones, son of John Jones of Moor Land and Mary his wife, was born near 4:00 in the morning 24 Nov 1748 being Thursday in Moor Land.

Hannah Dungan, dau of Thomas Dungan of Warminster and Esther his wife, was born 24 Sep 1725 about 6:00 in the afternoon in Warminster being Friday.

Elizabeth Dungan, dau of Thomas Dungan of Warminster and Esther his wife, was born 11 Jan 1727/8 near 9:00 in the morning in Warminster.

Thomas Dungan, son of Thomas Dungan of Warminster and Esther his wife, was born near midnight 31 Jan 1729/30 in Warminster.

Sarah Dungan, dau of Thomas Dungan of Warminster and Esther his wife, was born 13 Nov 1731 in Warminster.

Abel Dungan, son of Thomas Dungan of Warminster and Esther his wife, was born 26 May 1734 in Warminster.

Daniel Dungan, son of Thomas Dungan of Warminster and Esther his wife, was born 22 Apr 1736 in Warminster.

Enoch Dungan, son of Thomas Dungan of Warminster and Esther his wife, was born 11 Sep 1739 in Warminster.

Benjamin Dungan, son of Thomas Dungan of Warminster and Esther his wife, was born near 3:00 in the afternoon 16 Jul 1743 in Warminster.

Josiah Hart, fourth son of Joseph Hart of Warminster and Elizabeth his wife, was born between 10 and 11 o'clock afternoon 17 Jul 1749 being Monday.

Eleanor Hart, dau of Oliver Hart of Warminster (but at present residing in Charles Town, SC) was born at or near 3:00 in the afternoon 22 May 1750 in Warminster.

Elijah Jones, son of John Jones of Moor Land and Mary his wife, was born about 10:00 afternoon 20 Feb 1750/51 Wednesday in Moor Land.

Elizabeth Jones, dau of John Jones of Moor Land and Mary his wife, was born about 1:00 in the morning 6 Aug 1753 being Monday in Moor Land.

Ann Jones, dau of John Jones of Moorland and Mary his wife, was born about 2:00 afternoon 24 May 1755 being Saturday in Moor Land.

Joseph Hart, the sixth son of Joseph Hart of Warminster and Elizabeth his wife, was born about 8:00 in the morning 7 Dec 1758 being Thursday in Warminster.

Sarah Gilbert, dau of John Gilbert (of Moorland Township, Phila Co) and Mary his wife, was born 30 Dec 1734 in Moorland.

Phebe Gilbert, dau of John Gilbert and Mary his wife, was born 11 Sep 1736 in Moorland.

Rebeckah Gilbert, dau of John Gilbert and Mary his wife, was born 29 Mar 173[illegible] in Moorland.

Mary Gilbert, dau of John Gilbert and Mary his wife, was born 21 May 1741 in Moorland.

Jonathan Gilbert, son of John Gilbert and Mary his wife, was born 13 Jun 1743 in Moorland.

Joshua Gilbert, son of John Gilbert and Mary his wife, was born 2 Jun 1746 in Moorland.

Mercy Gilbert, dau of John Gilbert and Mary his wife, was born 19 Feb 1749/50 in Moorland.

John Gilbert, son of John Gilbert and Mary his wife, was born 6 Feb 1752 between 11 and 12 o'clock afternoon being Thursday in Moorland.

Jane Gilbert, dau of John Gilbert and Mary his wife, was born 29 Jan 1754 being Tuesday.

Jesse Gilbert, son of John Gilbert and Mary his wife, was born 10 May 1757 about 8:00 in the morning being Tuesday in Moorland.

Martha Gilbert, dau of John Gilbert and Mary his wife, was born 8 Nov 1759 between 11 and 12 o'clock afternoon being Thursday in Warminster.

Elias Yerkes, son of Silas Yerkes and Hannah his wife, was born about 1:00 in the morning 7 Dec 1751 being Saturday in Warwick Township.

Deborah Yerkes, dau of Silas Yerkes and Hannah his wife, was born near 3:00 in the morning 3 Sep 1753 being Monday in Warminster.

Esther Yerkes, second dau of the above named Silas and Hannah, was born about 5:00 in the morning 13 Feb 1755 being Thursday in Warwick.

Thomas Yerkes, second son of Silas and Hannah above named, was born about 4:00 in the morning 24 Sep 1756 being Friday in Warwick.

Elizabeth Yerkes, the third dau of Silas and Hannah above named, was born about 3:00 in the afternoon 26 Mar 1758 being Easter Sunday in Warwick.

John Yerkes, the third son of Silas and Hannah above named, was born near 4:00 in the morning 26 Sep 1760 in Mooreland.

Thomas Hough, son of Isaac Hough & Edith his wife of Warminster, was born 7 Oct 1761.

Oliver Hough, son of said Isaac Hough was born on 27 Aug 1763.
Silas Hough was born 8 Feb 1766.
Joseph Hough was born 17 Jun 1768.
William Hough was born 12 Sep 1770.
John Gilbert, son of Nicholas Gilbert and his wife Sarah, decd, was born 30 Mar 1711.
Mary Gilbert, dau of said Nicholas Gilbert and Sarah his wife, was born 23 Nov 1714.
Samuel Gilbert, son of the said Nicholas Gilbert and Sarah his wife, was born 8 Nov 1716.
Jacob Gilbert, son of the said Nicholas and Sarah, was born 19 Jul 1718.
Joseph Gilbert, son of the said Nicholas and Sarah, was born 17 Nov 1720.
Benjamin Gilbert, son of the said Nicholas and Sarah, was born 26 Jun 1722.
Peter Gilbert, son of the said Nicholas and Sarah, was born 25 Nov 1726.
Nathan Banes, son of Thomas Banes of Southampton and Jane his wife, was born about 8:00 in the night 3 Jun 1740 being Tuesday.
Isaac Banes, son of the said Thomas Banes and Jane his wife, was born about 1:00 in the morning 17 Feb 1741/2 being Wednesday.
Thomas Banes, son of the said Thomas Banes and Jane his wife, was born about 5:00 in the afternoon 3 Oct 1744 being Wednesday.
Stephen Banes, son of the abovesaid Thomas Banes and Jane his wife, was born about 6:00 in the afternoon 8 Jul 1753 being Sunday.
Jane Banes, dau of the said Thomas Banes and Jane his wife, was born about 2:00 in the morning 8 Dec 1758 being Friday in Southampton.
Joseph Shaw, son of John Shaw of Northampton and Elizabeth his first wife, decd, was born 5 Mar 1725 about 3:00 afternoon being Saturday in Northampton.
Elizabeth Shaw, dau of the said John Shaw and Elizabeth, was born 9 Mar 1730 at 10:00 in the forenoon being Saturday in Northampton.
James Shaw son of the said John Shaw and Sarah his second wife, was born 3 Dec 1733 about 6:00 in the morning being Monday in Northampton.
John Shaw, son of the said John Shaw and Sarah his wife, was born 10 Mar 1738/9 about 4:00 in the afternoon being Saturday in Northampton.
Jonathan Shaw, son of the said John Shaw and Sarah his wife, was born 18 Feb 1748/9 about 6:00 afternoon being Saturday in Northampton.
Deborah Dungan, dau of Thomas Dungan of Warwick and Mary his wife, was born about 3 or 4 o'clock in the morning 25 May 1731 in Warwick.
Joseph Dungan, son of the above named Thomas Dungan and Mary his wife, was born about 8:00 in the morning 13 Apr 1736 in Warwick.
Lucretia Dungan, dau of Thomas and Mary afsd, was born about 10:00 in the morning 16 Aug 1740 in Warwick.

Jonathan Dungan, son of Thomas and Mary afsd, was born about 4:00 afternoon 4 Oct 1743 in Warwick.

Hannah Dungan, dau of Thomas and Mary afsd, was born about 4:00 in the morning 15 Apr 1745 in Warwick.

John Dungan, son of Thomas and Mary afsd, was born about 8:00 in the morning 25 Dec 1746 in Warwick.

Abel Morgan, son of Randal Morgan and Grace his wife of Moorland was born about half an hour after 1:00 afternoon in Moorland in 1737.

Enoch Morgan, son of Randal and Grace above named, was born about midnight between 13 & 14 Dec 1739 in Southampton.

Grace Morgan, dau of Randal Morgan and Grace his wife, was born 30 Apr 1742 in the evening.

Ann Morgan, dau of the said Randal Morgan and Grace his wife, was born 5 Dec 1744 in the morning.

Mary Morgan, dau of the said Randal Morgan and Grace his wife, was born 20 Sep 1751 in the morning.

Randal Morgan, the youngest son of Randal Morgan and Grace his wife abovesaid, was born 25 Oct 175- in the morning.

Thomas Craven, son of Peter Craven and Mary his wife, was born 24 Oct 1756 about 1:00 afternoon in Southampton being Sunday.

Ann Craven, dau of Peter Craven and Mary afsd, was born 4 Jul 1758 near 4:00 in the afternoon being Tuesday in Warminster.

John Craven, the second son of Peter Craven and Mary abovesaid, was born 11 Sep 1760 between 8 and 9 o'clock afternoon being Thursday in Warminster.

Mary Hart, dau of the Revd Mr. Oliver Hart & Sarah his wife, was born 6 Sep 1762 in Charles Town, SC.

Grace Morgan, dau of Abel Morgan and Mary Morgan, was born 24 Jun 1766 about 10:00 in the morning.

William Morgan, son of the said Abel Morgan & Mary his wife, was born on Friday 2 Jun 1769 between 6 & 7 o'clock in the evening.

Josiah Dungan, son of Joseph Dungan and Elizabeth his wife, was born in Warwick 29 Jan 1765 about 3:00 in the morning.

Thomas Dungan, son of the said Joseph Dungan of Warwich and Elizabeth his wife, was born 9 Aug 1767 about 2:00 in the afternoon

James Dungan, son of the said Joseph Dungan and Elizabeth his wife, was born 1 Jun 1769 about 9:00 in the morning.

John Dungan, son of the said Joseph and Elizabeth, was born 5 Jul 1771.

Willliam Van Horne son of Revd Peter P. Van Horne & Margaret his wife and Lavinia Budd Daughter of Thomas Budd & Jamima his wife of Northampton, Burlington Co, West Jersey were joined together in the

Holy Bands of Matrimoney 1 Dec 1772 by Revd Samuel Jones. Their issue:

Anne Van Horne born 13 Dec 1773 in Southampton.
Margaret Van Horne born Apr 1775 being Easter Sunday.
Elizabeth Van Horne born 14 Dec 1776 in Southampton.
Mary Van Horne born 3 Oct 1778 in Southampton.
Lavinia Van Horne born 27 Jul 1781 in Southampton.
Thomas Budd Van Horne born 1 Jul 1783 in Southampton.

A Register of Births the Parents Not Being Members

Rachel Stephenson, dau of James Stephenson of Moorland and Martha his wife, was born 5 Feb 1744.

Thomas Dungan, son of John Dungan of Northampton and Sarah his wife, was born 29 Mar 1743 at 12:00 at night.

James Dungan, son of the said John and Sarah, was born 7 Apr 1747 at 4:00 afternoon. He died in Feb 1748/9.

John Dungan, son of the said John and Sarah was born 12 Jan 1748/9 at 4:00 in the morning.

Joseph Dungan, son of the said John and Sarah, was born 26 Jul 1752 at 3:00 afternoon being Sunday.

Hannah Hart, the second dau of Oliver Hart and Sarah his wife, was born 6 Dec 1752 about 3:00 in the afternoon being Wednesday in Charles Town, SC. She died 2 Sep 1753 in Charles Town.

Jesse Dungan, son of John Dungan and Sarah his wife, above name, was born 22 Oct 1754 about 11:00 in the forenoon being Tuesday.

Oliver Hart, the second son of Oliver Hart and Sarah his wife, abovenamed, was born 7 Nov 1754 about 5:00 in the morning being Thursday in Charles Town.

Isaac Dungan, son of John Dungan and Sarah his wife, above named, was born 9 Jan 1758 about 6:00 in the morning being Monday.

John Hart, the third son of Oliver Hart and Sarah his wife above named, was born 6 Mar 1758 at 5:00 in the afternoon being Monday in Charles Town.

Joseph Hart, the fourth son of Oliver and Sarah above named, was born about 5:00 afternoon on Wednesday 12 Nov 1760 in Charles Town, S.C.

Eleanor Hough, dau of Isaac Hough of Warminster and Edith his wife, was born 2 Aug 1749 about 3:00 afternoon being Wednesday in Warminster.

Elizabeth Hough, dau of the said Isaac and Edith, was born 21 Aug 1751 about 7:00 afternoon being Wednesday in Warminster.

Susannah Hough, dau of the said Isaac and Edith, was born 28 Jun 1753 about 3:00 in the afternoon being Thursday in Warminster.

John Hough, son of the said Isaac and Edith, was born 12 Mar 1755 near 4:00 in the afternoon being Wednesday in Warminster.

Mary Hough, dau of Isaac and Edith above named, was born about 12 hours afternoon 19 May 1757 being Thursday in Warminster.

Isaac Hough, second son of Isaac and Edith above named, was born about 2:00 in the morning 15 Sep 1759 being Friday in Warminster.

Thomas Hough, the third son of Isaac and Edith above named, was born about 10:00 at night 7 Oct 1761 being Wednesday in Warminster.

Seth Gilbert, the first son of William Gilbert of Warminster and Lucretia his wife, was born near 11:00 afternoon 18 Mar 1742/3 being Friday in Warminster.

Silas Gilbert, the second son of William and Lucretia abovenamed, was born at 9:00 afternoon 2 Mar 1745/6 being Sunday in Warminster.

Joseph Gilbert, third son of William and Lucretia abovenamed, was born near 8:00 in the morning 9 Oct 1748 being Sunday in Warminster.

John Thomas, first son of John Thomas and Lucretia his wife (late w/o William Gilbert abovenamed) was born about 12:00 afternoon 31 Jan 1753 being Wednesday in Cheltenham, Phila Co.

Elizabeth Thomas, first dau of John Thomas and Lucretia his wife above named, was born at 4:00 afternoon 8 Mar 1755 being Saturday in Cheltenham, Phila Co.

Isaac Thomas, second son of John and Lucretia above named, was born at 8:00 afternoon 13 Nov being Sunday in Cheltenham, Phila Co. He died 11 Oct 1760.

Eleanor Thomas, second dau of John and Lucretia above named, was born about 6:00 in the morning 3 Dec 1759 being Monday in Cheltenham, Phila Co.

William Hart, son of John Hart & Rebekah his wife, was born in Southampton 9 Sep 1768. Died 8 Dec 1769.

William Hart, second son of the said John & Rebekah Hart, was born at Southampton 11 Apr 1770.

Joseph Hart, third son of the said John & Rebekah Hart, was born in the Borough of Chester 17 Nov 1771.

Euphemia Hart, second dau of the said John & Rebecka, was born at Chester afsd 22 Dec 1775.

John Hart, fourth son of the said John & Rebekah, was born in Warminster, Bucks Co 19 Oct 1777.

Isaac Craven, son of Thomas Craven Junr and Elioner his wife, was born in Warwick, Bucks Co 29 Sep 1767.

Edith Craven, dau of the afsd Thomas & Elioner, was born 7 Oct 1768 in Warwick.

Abner Craven, 2nd son of the said Thomas & Elioner, was born 11 Dec 1767 in Warwick.

Burials

Lucy Chamberlin died about midnight or after 18 Apr 1747 and was buried at Southampton the 20th aged about 87 years.

John Harrison died near 10:00 at night 27 May 1748 and was buried at Southampton the 29th aged about [blank].

Elizabeth Morford died 11 Nov 1748 in the morning. Buried at Southampton the 13th. Aged about 35 ½ years.

Samuel Gilbert died 7 Mar 1749/50 in the morning and was buried at Southampton the 9th. Aged near 62 years.

Sarah Murray died 3 Apr 1752 in the morning with a fall from a horse of which she died immediately. Buried at Southampton the 5th. Aged near 53 years.

John Eaton died 3 Oct 1753 in the morning and was buried at Southampton the 5th. Aged about 52 years 9 months.

Thomas Potts died at his house in West Jersey 2 Feb 1754 and was buried at Burdentown the 4th. Aged 76 years 1 month.

Joanna Gilbert died 11 Aug 175- in the morning and was buried at Southampton the 13th. Aged about 86 years.

Eleanor Hart died between 12 and 1 o'clock in the morning 29 Oct 1754 and was buried the next day at Southampton. Aged about 67 years 5 weeks.

Susannah Thomas died about 2:00 afternoon 27 Jul 175- and was buried the 29th at Southampton. Aged 50 years 2 months.

Martha Eaton died about midnight between 28 and 29 Sep 1756 and was buried at Southampton the 30th. Aged 52 years 1 month.

Elizabeth Yerkes died 11 Oct 17-- and was buried at Pennepack the 13th. Aged 68 years 6 months.

Grace Morgan died 20 Dec 1757 in the morning and was buried the next day at Southampton. Aged 41 years 3 months.

Mary Jones died 29 Aug 175- in the afternoon and was buried at Southampton the 31st. Aged 43 years 10 months 6 days.

Thomas Dungan of Warminster died between 11 and 12 o'clock at night 20 Jan 1759 and was buried at Southampton the 23rd. Aged 68 years 4 months.

Thomas Dungan of Northampton died 23 Jun 1759 in the morning and was buried at Southampton the next day. Aged a little more than 88 years. He was uncle to Thomas Dungan above.

Mary Parry a Negro died 11 Nov 1760 and was buried at Southhampton the next day. Aged about [blank].

Robert Parsons died 30 Nov 1760 in the evening and was buried 3 Dec following at Southampton. Aged about 82 or 83 years.

Rachel Dungan died 20 Mar 1761 and was buried at Southampton. Aged 42 years 2 months.

Sarah Stephens died between the 26 & 27 Mar 1761 and was buried at the Society the 28th. Aged near 37 years.

Jeremiah Dungan of Northampton died 6 Apr 1861 and was buried at Southampton the 8th. Aged about 88 years.

Joshua Potts the first ordained minister of the Church at Southampton died at his own house in Moorland about 4:00 18 Jun 1761 and was buried at Southampton the 20th. Aged 42 years 5 months 14 days.

John Jones died about 10:00 before noon 26 Nov 1761 and was buried at Southampton the 29th. Aged 59 years 10 months.

David Rees Departed this Life and was buried at Southampton the next day 13 May 1762. Aged about 49 years.

Nicholas Gilbert Departed this Life and was buried at Southampton 8 May 1762. Aged 80 years 7 months.

John Hart Departed this Life and was buried at Southampton 27 Mar 1763. Aged [blank].

Martha Ferriby widow Departed this Life and was buried at Southampton the next day 23 Dec 1772. Aged about 50 years.

Elizabeth Sands widow and relict of Richard Sands Departed this Life and was buried at Southampton. Aged about 50 years.

Elioner Beans spinster & sister to the above named Elizabeth S. Departed this Life and was buried at Southampton 30 Apr 1773. Aged about 49 years.

William Folwell departed this life and was buried at Southampton 4 Jun 1776. Aged 72 years.

Sarah Shaw wife of John Shaw departed this life and was buried at Southampton. Aged [blank].

John Shaw departed this life and was buried at Southampton. Aged [blank].

Mary Davis departed this life and was buried at [blank].

Rachel Prichard departed this life and was buried at Southampton 2 Nov 1780. Aged 71 years.

Isaac Hough departed this life and was buried at Southampton. Aged [blank].

Elizabeth Hart departed this life and was buried at Southampton 19 Feb 1788.

Ann Folwell departed this life and was buried at Southampton 20 Feb 1788. Aged 81 years 6 months.

Joseph Hart esqr departed this life and was buried at Southampton 1788. Aged 72 years 5 months 24 days.

Sarah Watts departed this life and was buried at Southampton 3 Feb 1791. Aged [blank].

Anthony Yerkes departed this life and was buried at Southampton 9 Mar 1791.

Mary Dungan departed this life and was buried at Southampton 23 Jul 1793.

Hannah McNeal departed this life and was buried at Southampton 17 Feb 1794. Aged [blank].

Elizabeth Watts departed this life and was buried at Southampton 16 Mar 1794. Aged 87 years.

John Gilbert departed this life and was buried at Southampton. Aged [blank].

Christiana Banes departed this life and was buried at Penepack 11 Nov 1794. Aged [blank].

Silas Yerkes died and was buried at Southampton 23 Sep 1794.

Stephen Watts of Southampton & there buried.

Ann Folwell dau of Wm & Ann afsd.

Silas Hart died 31 Dec 1795 aged 74 years 5 months 24 days.

Oliver Hart died 31 Dec 1795 aged 72 years 5 months 26 days.

A REGISTER OF MEMBERS RECEIVED BY LETTERS FROM OTHER CHURCHES.

Esther Dungan, wife of Thomas Dungan of Warminster, by a letter of the 13 June 1747 from the Church at Montgomery. Received on 20th of same month.

Jane Griffith, member of the Church at Lower Dublin by a letter from the same church of 5 Nov 1748, received as a member 18 Dec 1748.

Samuel Guy and his wife Rebeckah, by a letter of recommendation, and dismission from the church at Lower Dublin. Received as a member 15 April 1749.

Mary Davis, wife of Thomas Davis of Horsham, was received as a member on 15 Dec by letter from the church at Lower Dublin, dated 1 Sep 1754.

Martha Eaton, widow of John Eaton, by a letter of the 9th of this instant from the Church at Montgomery was received as a member on 15 March 1755.

William Folwell and Ann his wife, by a letter of 10 May last from the church at Middletown and Crossswick in the Jersies, were received as members on 20 July 1755.

Joseph Richardson and Mary his wife by a letter from the church at Lower Dublin of 5 June last were received on 21 Aug 1757.

Grace Webster was received by examination on 6 May 1764. She had formerly been baptized and a member amongst the 7th Day Baptists.

The Rev. Wm. Vanhorn was dismissed to us from the church at Penepack alias Lower Dublin by a letter dated 7 May 1772. He had been a Probationer for some time, and being well approved of, on 30th of the same month he was ordained to the great work of a Gospel minister by Revd. Mr. Isaac Eaton and James Jones.

Erasmus Kelley was dismissed to us from the church at Philadelphia and rec'd. by us 5 Jan 1778.

Mr. William Vanhorn was received a member by a letter from the church at Penepack alias Lower Dublin.

Mary Meghee was received as a member with us by a letter from the church at Upper Freehold, NJ on 12 Dec 1784. Revd. David Jones was dismissed from the church at Great Valley and rec'd by us on 25 March 1786.

Elizabeth Watts was dismissed from the church at Upper Freehold and received into Union with us on 28 May 1787.

William W. Folwell, son of Thos. Folwell was recd. into the church fellowship on 10 Aug 1794 upon his letter of recommendation and dismission from the church at Providence Rhode Island.

On 12 Oct 1794 Thomas Meminger, a licensed preacher, was recd. into church fellowship upon a letter of recommendation and dismission from the church at Jacobs Town, NJ.

A REGISTER OF MEMBERS DISMISSED BY LETTERS

16 Oct 1748 Isaac Eaton being removed to Hopewell in Hunterdon Co., in West Jersey.

18 Dec 1749. James Dungan to the church at Lower Dublin.

19 Aug 1749. Elizabeth Baldin to the church at Lower Dublin.

14 July 1750. Hannah Smith, formerly Watts, being by her marriage removed and settled in Philadelphia.

21 April 1754. Mary Griffith, formerly Coffing, was dismissed to the church at Montgomery.

17 Oct 1756. Mary —, formerly Newman was dismissed to the church at — in VA.

17 Dec 1758. Rebeckah Humphrys being gone to live with her father, requested to be dismissed to Montgomery (that being much nearer for her than Southampton.

19 Aug 1759. Hannah Burns was dismissed to the church at Montgomery.

3 May 1772. Abel Morgan was dismissed to the church at Penepack.

5 July 1766. Ann Potts, widow and relict of the Rev. Joshua Potts late minister of his place, dec'd., was dismissed to the church at Croswicks.

5 May 1768. Soon after this Thomas Dungan, son of Joseph Dungan, was dismissed to the First Baptist Church at Philadelphia.

2 May 1772. Abel Morgan was dismissed to the Church at Lower Dublin Pennypack.

12 June 1784. Isaac Hough, Junr. was dismissed to the church at Lower Dublin Pennypack.

12 June 1784. Isaac Hough Junr. was dismissed to the church at Pennepeck afterwards excommunicated.

11 Oct 1789. Elinor Craven, formerly Hough, was dismissed to the church at Cetocton(?) in VA.

3 April 1792. Revd. David Jones and two daus. Elinor and Mary were dismissed to the church at Great Valley from whence they came.

15 Sep 1792. Mr. Benjamin Bennet, a licensed Preacher, was dismissed to the church at Middletown, NJ.

20 Sep 1795. Nancy Taylor and Abigail Curtis were dismissed to the Baptist church in Philadelphia.

A REGISTER OF MEMBERS EXCOMMUNICATED OR DISOWNED

16 July 1749. John Baldwin, being accused of Drinking to excess, was twice sent to by the Church to come and clear himself, but he absolutely refused to come to the Church... he lived in a continued course of drunkenness...

20 July 1755. Hannah Burns was publickly excommunicated for fornication.

19 June 1762. Conrad Smith having for a long time absented himself from the Communion of the Church ... and declared he never intended to return.

16 Oct. Thomas Beans for obstinacy and falsely reproaching several of the Brethren.

7 July 1765. Samuel Guy and his wife Rebecka. See the Church minutes.

5 March 1769. John Morford and his wife Margaret. See the minutes.

30 Dec 1769. Joseph Richardson.

14 Aug 1774. James Bray for disorderly walking, neglect of his place in the Church.

16 June 1781. James Dungan.

5 Jan 1794. Harry, a Negro man.

1799. John Hough.

MEMORANDA FROM THE DIARY OF JOHN DYER OF PLUMSTEAD, BUCKS COUNTY, PENNSYLVANIA

The complete "Memoranda From the Diary of John Dyer of Plumstead, Bucks Co., PA." was published in *The Pennsylvania Genealogical Magazine*. Volume III (1906). Following are excerpts pertaining to marriages and deaths. The dates are sometimes difficult to determine.

16 Nov 1763 Father's family moved to MD---

1 Mar 1764 Butlers moved to fathers place
6th Joseph Riches son Jon. B.
9th Mary Shaw Departed this Life 9 Jun 1764 and was buryed the 10th in the afternoon---
23rd in the afternoon Set Wm. Preston Departed this life
7th this morning Isaac Fell Hanged him Self in his own Barn
14th about 6:00 this Evening Wm Reders house was struck with Lightning & several people were very much hurt. Joseph Watson & Robert Kirkbride being not able to be moved home.
17th Kirbride was moved home--- Watson being gon a Day or two---
19th Elizabeth Elicott Departed this Life about 1:00 this morning of the small pox
23rd Arthur Allen Dyed of a Consump
6 18 Edward Good was married to Eleanor Harris at Joh Browns
2 Wm & John Grifeth from England was at Plumsted
12-31 Frances Dawes married to Mary

1767
3-5 & 6 Surveyers & Jury on the Line & between 30 & 40 other people at the Line and Corner between Father and Wm. Erwin
3 21 appointed to chose Supervisors for the high ways between 2 & 5 oclock Hugh Farguson Jno Carey
4-2 Isaac Brown's vandue---
4-3 John Child moved to Logan place near Garmantown
4-4 Isaacs took some goods to the place he bought of David Smith---
4-6 Isaac Brown moved from my place---
4-13 Benjn Brittan moved to my place---
4-17 A stone set for a corner by Wm Buckman Sheriff in the presents of William Bradfield Alxr Brown John Carlile Benjamin Brittan Joseph Butler John Miers Shoemaker Samuel Anderson & Wm Rich
17 23 Mary Dillon married to Joseph Kenerd over the River I sopose
5-4 at night James Hart tavern keeper Dyed of pleurisy
5-21 Thomas Goode married to Ester Lewis at her own house

6 3 William George Departed this Life in the Evening being about 97 years of age
6 27 Alexr Brown's Jur Barn Raised
6-30 Henry Jemison Keepar Departed this Life in the afternoon
8 24 Robert Stuart and three of his Sons Struck Dead with a vapor or sulphur in his well this morning there was such a Damp or Sulphery vapor in Robert Stuarts well that it killd him & three of his Sons one of them Going Down to Doo Something in the well fell down Dead as they sopose and the rest Going Down one by one Expecting to help them that were Down but fell Down Dead as fast as they came to the bottom, another man named Snotgrass was let Down and Drawed up again as Quick as posable but was so far Gon that he Did not come too for an hour or there abouts.
8 25 In the afternoon they were buried in one grave
9 9 Andrew Ellicott and Esther Brown married by Gilbert Hicks Esqr at Andrews one house 9 Sep 1767 in Plumpstead

1768
3-19 Hugh Fergason and James Shaw chose Supervisers for the highways this year
4-13 Buckingham meeting house Burned to the Ground
6 26 or before this Hette Elicotts son born
7-3 Kirkbrides servant John Gill Died with Drinking Cold water when hot 2 weeks before---
7 18 Thomas George set of for MD for money his Legacy 39£ or 13 hf.
8-17 Parcilla Child wife of Cephas Child Departed this Life
11 9 Ben. Brittain moved for VA

1769
1 5 Came home to plumpstead and the same night I was married
2 22 Solomon Willits was here on his way to VA
3 12 Benjamin Brown was here from the Great medows
3 29 John Naylor Junr was here from MD
4 5 Isaac Child departed this life of a short Illness---
4-7 Isaac Child Buryed this Day. He was a worth man I think & a preacher of the Gospel.
5-6 John Scarborough Departed this Life Last night about 9:00 of a palsey
5 7 and was buryed this Day where was above a thousand people I believe the Largest Ever I saw he was a worthy Minister of the Gospel many years and I think will be much missed.
6 11 the 11th day of Jun between 9 & 10 o'clock in the morning Elizabeth Dyer was born

6 22 Vandue of Peter Vickers Estate had by the assignees Jon & Thos Dyer for the use of his Creditors
7 2 Daniel White Dyed of a very short Illness---Last night being abroad in the Evening and dyed in the morning.
7 19 Martha Hayter widow departed this Life last Night
7 24 John Ewers was buryed this day but when he Dyed I'm not Sure---
8 13 This day Thomas Furness came here from MD
8 28 Rachel Willson was a Plumstead from old England a noted preacher approved I believe by all Sorts of people
9 1 Martha Kinsey Died of a Consumption and was buryed ye 2nd
9 21 Cornelious Hillyards folks set off for VA &
9 22 Jane Carrol set off home to VA
10 6 Benja. Foster Came from VA
11 5 Edward Doyl Departed this life about Noon
12-19 Joseph Wright born about 1:00 this morning
12-29 Joseph Fell's wife departed this Life & was
12-31 buryed at Buckingham 31st of Dec

1770
1 8 Nathaniel Brittains son had his Skull mashed to pieces by a kick from a horse
1 10 Alexr Brown married
1 11 Nathaniel Brittains son Died of the kick Recd a few days ago
1 17 Alexr Brown Jr. married this Day week past to Elizabeth Kinsey took her home this day
3 5 Computed to be 4474 houses in Philadelphia
3-11 Subscription for relief of Bartholomew Bolderson who had the misfortune to have house & shop burned to the ground---
8 14 John Hughes buryed this Day and I sopose he Died yesterday of a Dropsey
3 19 Elizabeth Farguson died last Night at Magills of a consumption---
3-17 Jonathan Shaw and Ezekil Roders Chose Supervisors for the highways for the ensuing year
3 21 Jeremiah Doyl moved away from our place---
3 26 Joseph Brown assigned over his Estate to Daniel Stradling & Andrew Ellicott for the use of his creditors
3 30 the Last Day but one of Mar Laurance Growdon Died who was Clark of the Court and one of the Governors Council.
4-21 Simon Meredith's house burnt this morning
5 8 Mark Day married to Sirfette [?]
5 15 James Latta, Minister from Deep Run moved to Chestnut Level I believe in Lancaster Co

5 16 David Copland moved towards VA with his family
5 17 Thomas Russel moved to VA Roder's Son in law---
7 10 News of Thomas Funress's Death about 6 weeks ago
10 8 Jacob Stiner married
10 30 Alexr Browns Daughter born
11 1 the master moved up to the place where Jere Doyl formerly lived & mother and Rachel with them
11 5 John Miers married this Day---
11 6 Joseph Lunn was killed by a wagon Running over his head which mashed it to pieces & he Dyed instantly almost as I understand
11-27 Josiah Dyers wife Rachel departed this Life 27 Nov late at night or soon the 28th in the morn and was buryed the 29th
12-22 Young Josiah Fenton Died last night of a shot in his hand.

1771
1 7 Father, Mother, Elizabeth & Rachel set for MD
1 8 Eliza married
1 24 John Reiley married to Roland ---
2 13 Joseph Rich had 2 sons Born
2-23 Wm. Riches son born
2-27 Hester Dyer was born 27 Feb 1771 about 4:00 in the afternoon
3-3 Mark Days Daughter born---
3-19 Ely Welding buryed this Day who Died of a swelling or wen on his neck or face he died 17 Mar in afternoon
3 29 Thos Polton set for MD and took Brittains Bond to Jon Dyer
4-22 Dawson Brown moved for VA
4-27 Ambros Barcrafts wife hanged herself.
4-28 Hester Dyer Junr went to keep house for Josiah
4 29 Mathew Day moved to MD
5 6 Wm. Reeder & Jas Love set off for VA with their famalys John and Gourley keeps the tavern where Reeder kept it
5 6 Thos Polton & Bet moved to his place this Day
5 16 Andrew Ellicott set of for Baltimore to build a mill at Elk Ridg
6 8 Ann Furness and her son Thomas came here from Peters Borrough, York Co.
7 10 Jacob Stiners Daughter born
7 21 Polton's son born Last Night
8 8 John Myers son born last night
8 23 Last night Charles Polton had two sons born, one of them is Dead and the other Died in 2 or 3 Days
8 27 Sarah Rich was married to W. Wood this evening by Benjamin Mathews Esqr

9-1 Samuel Neal was a Plumstead & preached a fine Sermon, he came from Ireland
9 23 John Hough died this night
9 27 Josiah Brown chosen asseser this Day
9 28 Benjamin Cutlers Daughter Born---
10-8 Sarah Rich or Wood's Daughter born this Day
10 10 Mary Wrights daughter born last night about 9:00
Richard Penn Esqr our Governer arrived in Philadelphia this Day
10 29 Wm. Wood & Sarah Wood moved to Carrs---
11 21 Martha Brown married to Wm. Shoemaker
12-26 Jane Anderson married to Jas Sample this Day.

1772
1 5 John Shokea's wife Died last night
1 9 Henry Stiner Died this day
1 27 a son of Geo. Newman perished in the snow
2-11 Clement Doyl was buryed this Day, but when he died I am not certain.
2 11 Joseph Townsend was buryed the same day
2-29 Sarah Shaw's Daughter born this morning, Alex. wife---
3 28 John Samuels a Dumb man was buryed this day
4-15 Wm. M'Calla moves this Day to Reeders tavern---
5 3 John Fells house and Shop was burnt Last night.
5 14 Doctor Meredith married
8 9 Alexander Browns Daughter born last night & Charles Poltons D. yesterday or last night
8 25 John Shokea married to Mary Stiner---
8 24 Hette Ellicotts son of Daughter born this morning
8 30 John Stiner came from MD & gave some account of John Moore
9 18 Rebecca Furness Died last night about 12:00
9 21 James Evans Died last night
9 25 Burall Moore & his wife was here this Day from VA
9 26 William Erwin Died last night after short illness---
9 27 Jo Hails wife had 2 Daughters born last night
9 29 Mary Dyer was born about 10:00 forenoon
10-8 Ephraim Evins son born this morning
10 26 John Shockea killed with a wagon about Noon this Day---
11 2 Poll Eaton's Daughter Polton born this Day
11 5 Titus Fell Died Last Night
11 20 George Walter was hurt by a fall from a horse last Night had his leg Broke & otherways bruised---
12-3 Sarah Watson Departed this Life this morning of a lingering illness or decay with age

12-15 John Stiner married Cate Sees or Russell
12-22 Abraham Freet Died last Night I soppose---
12 23 Levi Rich died this Day about 11:00 I believe
12-24 Nathaniel Sample married to one Su Bowers---
12 26 Peter Kelleys son born
12-29 Wm. Harkins's son born Last night
12-31 John Earls Died this Day about 3:00

1773
1 2 James McKenney's Child Died this evening
1 16 Joseph Riches son Jesse Dyed with the small pox this morning---
2-7 Abraham Tucker's Daughter Elizabeth died of the Small pox Last night---
2-7 Joseph Michiners Child Died of the Measels
2-16 Isaac Rich married to Ruth Polton this Day
2 18 Thos Poltons Daughter born this morning
2-25 George Brown & John Rogers and Alexr
2 26 Browns Children Anocalated for the Small pox
3-3 Samuel Kesters son born the first child
3 5 Wm. Woods daughter born about 6 this Evening
3 25 Jean Tyson Died of the Small pox at Joseph Brittains after she was published for marriage with Levy Fell
4 6 Felex Felle moved for MD with Mark Day his Son in Law
4-13 Joseph Butler moved from our place to Eldad Robertses near Edward Bartholomew's
4 19 A Letter dated from Bristol 25 Jan to his frd in Philadelphia Gives account of the Ships Phebe & peggy being wrecked near Millford in Wales & 18 people said to be Drowned
4-26 Surveyor and men on the line between Alben Thomas & Cephes Child: Joseph Hart Esqr James Wallace Esr Daniel Longstreth John Wilkinson Garrards Wynkoop & Rbt. Lollar Surveyer
4 29 Margret Erwin moved from here to her mothers this Day---
4 29 Last night or this Morning Eleazer Fenton had a son born
5 11 Little John Miller married to poll Mathews or poll Hough
5 12 Joseph Hough buried this Day at Buckingham the same Day Joseph Beal married to Hannah Russell at Saml Herolds
5 13 Nelle McAtee Buryed this Day in Philadelphia of Small pox as I understand---
14 Josha Dungin married to Elen H.
5 22 Mother & Phebe Moore came here this Evening from MD to Live I believe---
5 28 George Jewell's daughter named Alee (Bonn)

6 17 Mahlon Michiner married to Sarah Day
7 21 Abraham Tucker's son Born
8 2 Mary Shocke or Stiner married to Wm Meredith
8 7 John Browns son born last night about 1:00
8 7 George Michiner's Daughter born Last night about 11:00
9 4 David Eatons Daughter born yesterday morning
9 16 Stiners Daughter Born
10 12 John Gourley set off for Carolina with his family this Day
12 1 William Doyls wife Died this morning of a cancer in her Brest
12-6 John Moore was in this neighborhood to see his wife whom he Run away and Left some time ago to follow a Lude Girl of the name of Sarah Griffith
12-11 Isaac Riches Daughter born Last night

1774
1 23 Polle Rich Wms Daughter died this evening
2-11 James McKenneys son born Last night about 12:00
2-24 George James Died this morning of a short Illness being an old man about 78 years of age at Alben Thomases
3-25 Thos Wrights son Born
4-4 Joseph Michiner moved from his place this Day that he sold to Jonathan Shaw moved near Germantown
4-13 Thomas Dyer married to Sarah Preston
4 27 Joseph Burges moved for MD with his family
5 6 Johnne Browns daughter born this Day---
5-11 Mahlon Michiner's Daughter born
6 20 the 20th Day of Jun between 4-5 o'clock in the morning was born Joseph Dyer son of John & Jemima Dyers of Plumstead
7 18 Joseph Moores Daughter Sarah born this morning
7-23 Alexr Browns Daughter born
8 26 William Woods Daughter Mathilda was Scaulded to Death or so that she Died about 12 or 1 o'clock that night---
9-4 Robert Walker was a Plumstead, from old England
9 11 Poll Stiners Child Born
9 28 Hette Ellicott very much hurt by the Chair overseting
10 18 Alexr Shaw's Daughter Born
10-24 John West Departed this Life this morning of a fever
10 25 George Jewell's Daughter born this morning---
10 27 Wm. Woods Son born
10 29 Thos Poltons son born this morning
11 1 Peters Kelleys 2 Daughters born at 1 birth this Day

The association of the Congress now Come to hand they broke up or adjourned the 24th of Oct to some day in May next

11 11 Phebe Moores Daughter Susannah Died this afternoon---

11 21 Joseph Ellicott set off for MD with his family

12-12 George Fells wife Died Last night or this morning I believe

12-18 Nicholas Waln was at Plunstead this Day & preached, he formerly was a Lawyer

12 22 James Shaws Daughter married
Mary Shaw married to Wm. Bradsher or Bradshaw

12 23 John Vickers perished in the snow Last night, froze to Death near Roors Saw Mill

1775

1 1 Thos Dyers wife Delivered of a Son By Doctor Meredith 1 Jan

1 23 John Delaps wife died this morning

1 23 A daughter of Josiah fentons Died this morning of the small pox---

1 24 Isaac Thoms married to Sarah Brittain this Evening

1 29 James Meredith Died of a Cut received some time ago---

2-1 John Browns daughter Jane broke out with the small pox

2-16 This Day Eleazer Fentons Saw mill sawed the first

2-23 Jean Brown Departed this Life last night about 8:00

2-23 Jonathan Shaw's family & Alexr Shaws Anocalated for the small pox

2 24 Jean Brown buryed this Day

2 28 George Jewell moved from this town

8 6 Joseph Thos's Son born last night

3 9 Nance Wright went away---

3 11 Samuel Worthington Died this morning of a feaver

3 14 Daniel Evances wife Died last night of a fever

3 20 Thos Dyers wife & Child enocalated this Day

4 13 John Brown moved to Alexr's place

4 13 Wm Wood moved to Robert fishers

4-17 Robert Henderson Buryed, fever

4-20 Adam Shaver moved from Erwins place to place near Hudlestone

4-22 Little Rachel Wright Died of the small pox or worms Last night about 12:00

4-22 Bekke Black was here this Day the first of her return since she went to MD with Ellicotts to build their mill

5-6 Abraham Tyson buryed this Day with small pox

5 7 Little Thomas Wright Died of small pox this Evening about Dusk

5 8 Jonathan Worthington's wife died this Day of a fever a Nerves fever

6 17 Thomas Beal's wife died Last night about 12:00

7 20 this Day was appointed by the Congress (now seting at Philadelphia) a a Day of publick thanksgiving and prayer
George Washington is appointed Commander in Chief of the Continental Army & Charles Lee . . . . there has been a battle fought at Boston some time ago
7 21 this Day the Committee of this County met at Bogerts as also the Captains to Chuse their field officers as Colonels &c.
7 26 Hester Dyer married to John Bradshaw this Day where was about 100 people
7 27 Robert Gibson Married to Mary Brittain this day
8 14 Robert Poke was shot Dead this morning by accident as he and one Shannon was Exercising not knowing that the gun was Charged---
8 22 Ann Rich Departed this Life this morning of a Lingering Illness
9-5 Jonathan Goode married this Day to Simon Callenders Daughter
9 13 Joseph Riches Daughter born this morning
9 28 William Doyl married to Olive Hough this day
9 29 Nathaniel Brittain who fell in the well at Craigs old tavern some time ago and broke his Leg & otherways bruised himself was brought to the overseer of the poor of this township this Day
10 29 Samuel Harolds store broke open Last Night
11 1 Thomas Gill Departed this Life this morning about Day
11 23 Elizabeth Brown Daughter of Moses Brown deceasd long since married this Day to Abrm Paxon
12-4 Salle Brown married to Andrew Ellicott Junr at Newtown and Gon to MD to Live
12-6 Thos Wrights son born this morning
12-27 Jonathan Brown married to Rachel I sopose this Day

1776
1 19 Nathaniel Brittain Died last night
2-10 Mary Huett or Hughs Dyed this Day about 10:00 at Wm Doyls in Erwins house
2-20 Barack Michiner who married Christopher Days Daughter some time a Go, had two Children Born yesterday and one of them Died this Day
2-24 Alexander Brown Junr Departed this Life about 12:00 on the night of 23 Feb 1776 of a Consumption of which he was very poorly for a considerable time
2 24 Barack Michiners Wife Died about 5:00 this Evening the other Child Died some time afterwards
3 13 Zebelon Ashton of Wrightstown Died now abouts for he is to be Buried tomorrow at 10:00
3-13 James Bradshaw died this day I understand Great Military preparation

Made in America
3-19 John Chestnut moved from this town
3 21 Wm. Doyle moved to his lot that he bought of Arthur Erwin this Day
3 28 Peter Wood married to Peter Cosners Daughter
3 31 Thomas Gothrup was at Plumstead from old England, a man full of the holy Ghost preached a fine Sermon
4-24 Thomas Polton moved this Day
4-28 Hette Bradshaw's son Born this morning about 6
5 9 Bette polton's Daughter born last night
5 17 Alben Thomas Died last night after being Long poorly
5 22 Thos Wrights son Jesse Died this evening of fits
6 11 Richard Church Died this evening
6 17 Abraham Tucker moved for York Co over Susquehannah
7-8 was born John Dyer in the morning of 8 Jul about 1:00 1776, John Dyer was born, . . . son of John & Jemima Dyers
10 8 Jacob Walton to be buryed this Day I believe
11 3 Charles Polton Died this morning
11 6 Sall Eatons Daughter Born
11 17 Mahlon Kirkbride Senr Departed this Life this Day

1777
Daniel Penington Departed this Life this Day
2-20 Wm. Harkins Died of a fever
2-26 Joseph Fell Died this morning I believe
3 13 Jonathan Carlile married this Day
3 17 Joshua Gilbert Died last night of a fever & his mother a week before him
3-17 Mary Wrights son born this Day
5-15 John Brown married to Isaac Childs's widow this day at plumstead---
5 15 Samuel Herolds wife Died of a Consumption
5 15 I understand that Leah Ellicott Died this Day of Consumption
7 27 George Fell Died Last night---
8-11 I saw the American Army Encamped Near, or at the Cross Roads, Consisting of about 18,000 men in Bucks Co.
8 22 Robert Gibsons wife buryed this Day
8 23 Jonathan Hough's wife buryed this Day & Cornelious Shepard's yesterday & several children of the flux, I think I never knew so many people Die in so short a time, in this neighborhood
9 5 Thos Dyers son Jonas Died this Day about 7 or 8 o'clock in morning
9 10 John Brittains Wife Died this Day I believe of a Cancer
9 25 English entered Philadelphia 25 Sep
9 27 Robert Kirkbrides son Mahlon Died of a flux
10 4 Phebe Moores Daughter Rachel Died of the flux this evening

1778

4-24 Nathan Preston Departed this Life about 1:00 of the morning of 24 Apr 1778 and was buryed the 26th at Plumstead in the Compas of Ground where the old meeting hous stood attended by a vast number of people, by which it appeared that he was a man well beloved as a minister of the Gospel.

5-16 John Bradshaw a son of James Died this morning about Sun Rise---

5 29 Sarah Dyer Daughter of John & Jemima Dyer's was born between 1 & 2 o'clock in the morning of 29 May 1778.

6-18 The English Left Philadelphia 18 Jun 1778 with their army

1779

3-7 Jonathan Brown's son born 7 Mar

4-6 Hette Kirkbride married to Daniel Longstreth, a son this Day---

5 12 Daniel Thomas married to Hough in the night

10-14 Janne Brown married to John Beaumont

1780

1 22 Betse Brown Widdow married to Zenes Fell this Day

1 31 John Bradshaws son born about 11:00

4-16 About 1:00 16 Apr 1780 my aged father (about 72) Josiah Dyer Departed this Life very quietly after a long and tedious Illness being very poorly in MD before he came home & so Continued till his Departure

4-18 And was buryed the 18th at Plumstead

6 10 William Michiner Departed this Life about 3:00 this morning

7 2 Hezekiah Rogers Died this morning an old man

7 18 Was born Jemima Dyer Daughter of John & Jemima Dyers 18 Jul 1780

1782

6-1 Aaron Bradshaw Born

6-1 the first Day of Jun about 6:00 in the morning 1782 was Born Josiah Dyer son of John & Jemima Dyers of Plumstead

8 18 Granne Moore Uncle John Burroughs here

10-24 Joseph Moore moved to VA

11 2 Alexander Brown my uncle Departed this Life 2 Nov 1782 about 1:00 in the morning aged about 80

11 3 he was buryed where was a vast number of people

11 3 Mary Preston Died 3 Nov about sun rise of a Cancer in her Breast

11 17 James Kithins son born

12-2 Ephrim Evans Daughter Born

12-14 Wellses Daughter born

1783

1 31 Josiah Fenton Died

2 8 Martha Harvey Departed this Life this Evening about 7 or 8

2 25 Thomas Wright moved to Grinage

6 16 Thomas Dyer Esqr had a Son born this morning

6 19 John Shaw Departed this Life in the afternoon

6 21 Josiah Dyer son of John & Jemima Dyers Departed this Life about 9:00 on 21 Jun 1783

6 23 Elizabeth Dyer Daughter of John and Jemima of Plumstead, Departed this Life between 5 and 6 o'clock in the morning of 23 Jun 1783

6 24 And on 24 Jun our two infants were laid in one Grave

6 25 Wm. Rices wife Died this morning of small pox

7 5 Thomas Poltons son Charles Died this afternoon of the measles

8 27 Major Wm. Kenedy was wounded by the Robbers Last night

8 31 Major Kenedy Died of his wounds in the night of 31 Aug & was buryed with the honors of war on 2 Sep 1783---

9 23 We moved to the house I bought of Thos Wright

9 29 Thomas Shaws family set for VA with John Polton

10 15 James Kitchen moved for VA

10 18 Jonathan Wells set off for VA

10 18 Jonathan Riches son born same day John & his Daughter Ann was here from MD

12 7 Josiah Dyers Eldest Daughter Avis Departed this Life between the 6th & 7th

1784

4-8 George Shaws son born Apr 8

4-8 about half past four of the Clock P.M. my aged Mother (about 75) Hester Dyer Departed this Life on 8 Apr very Quietly and was Buryed the

4-11 Eleventh Day of the same

4-11 Josiah Dyer from the Great Medows Came here the same Morning to the burial 8 Apr Wrights moved from Greenage---

4-22 Josiah Brown Married to Deborah Willson this Day

5 29 Robert Fisher buryed this Day
Jonathan Hough Married 27 May

6 20 Joseph Fells wife Died

7 10 John Carey Jur's wife Died

8 3 Hannah Fenton Died

9-18 Ambras Polton killed on the hill as he was Diging sand, the bank caved on him & mashed him this afternoon

10-6 Robert Kirkbrides wife Departed this Life about 2:00 this morning of a short illness

10-8 And was buryed the 8th

10-9 Phebe Dyer daughter of John and Jemima Dyers of plumstead was born 9 Oct 1784

10 26 Wm. Rich fell in Jere Dungins Well about 25 feet as he was going to Go Down the Rope broke & he fell upon the bucket and Rock and

10 27 mashed his Brest so that he Died in the night of the 27th

10 28 John Brittain Departed this Life this Day, an aged man of good repute---

10 31 Olive Doyle Died this Day of a lingering disease

11 5 Samuel Wigton's eldest son mashed with a Cyder mill his arm & shoulder & brest so mashed that he Died the next Day that is this

11 6 Day

11 9 William Bradfield died last night I believe

11 20 Job Barton Died with a fall in the tailrace of Churches old mill---

11 30 Ephraim Evans moved above Durham furnace

12 11 Abraham Harvey buried this Day

1785

1 1 John Greer Died Last night of a fever

1 18 Philip Parry Buryed this Day

1 19 Barnet Swarts Wife buryed this Day

1 20 John Lock buryed this Day

2-20 Josiah Brown's son Born

4-14 the 14 Apr 1785, Aunt Esther Brown Departed this Life last night of a lingering Decay with age I believe, she was the Last of the old Stock of Browns & Dyers

4-16 and was buryed the 16 of sd month at Plumstead

4-25 Edward Moore moved

5 19 Amos Scott here from MD, Gave some acct of John Moore's moving to Juniatta

6 26 Edward Moores Child Died this morning about 1:00 of small pox

7 6 Phebe Dyer daughter of John & Jemima Dyer Departed this Life 6 Jul between 1 & 2 o'clock in the morning of the small pox

9 13 Sarah Carlile Departed this Life of a fever

9 13 Ezelil Hazel moved for Carolina with his family

10 22 John Preston Departed this Life about noon

11 1 Susannah Wells Departed this Life Last night suddenly

1786

1-18 Robert Kirkbride married to Hannah Willson

1 19 John Carey married to Eleanor Preston

3 3 Thomas Polton's son Born

3-11 John Bradshaws Daughter born

3-30 John Browns's Daughter born

4 6 Ludwick Thos Child & John Kasler moved this Day
5 29 Edward Moore's daughter born
6 8 Sall Poltons Daughter Born
9 19 Benjamin Day married to Isaac Hill's Daughter
12-28 The night of 28 Dec about 11:00 1786 was born Josiah 2nd Dyer son of John & Jemima Dyers of plumstead
12 30 Samuel Dyer and Rachel came from Sussex in NJ

1787
1 3 they set home again
1 16 Joseph Eaton's Wife Died of a Consumption
1 31 Thomas Watson Departed this Life this evening
2-2 Hugh Farguson's Wife and John Pickering Died about this time I understand
2-3 Thomas Watson buryed this Day
2-6 Jacob Winsmore Buryed this Day the oldest man in this part, between 107 & 108 years
2-9 Josiah Brown's Daughter born this Day
3 7 Captain Robert Gibson Jur Died this morning of a pluresy
4-5 George Show moved to the sign of the harrow to keep tavern
4 5 John Furness moved to this Town to Wm Doyls Lott
4-10 David Eaton and his family moved for MD
4-10 Jude Morton moved to our house with Mary Seamers
11 24 David Pugh Died suddenly by falling into a Spring about 4:00 this afternoon
11 29 Jesse Scott married to Rebeccah Jones (Jonathan Joneses Daughter)
12 26 Jonathan Riches wife (Rose) Hanged herself this morning in his one New Barn Built Last Summer

1788
1 10 Jesse Fell moved for Wyoming to Live
1 12 Daniel Thomase's Daughter born
1 15 John Worthingtons Daughter Born
1 23 Betts Hambletons son Born at John Bothers'es
1 30 Joseph Wright married to Sarah Kirkbride
3-9 Betts Preston's son Born
3 24 Isaac Willson married to Sale Brown
3-24 Joseph Sheperd married to Salle Carlile Last night; and William Child to Peggy Saunders this Day
4-3 Edward Moore moved away
4 6 Wm Doyl's Daughter Born
4-8 John Bother moved over the Run

4-10 John McCalla moved to Jonathan Brown's old place---
4-17 Matthias Brown married to Daniel Evan's Daughter
4-30 John Brown moved from plumstead to Chester Co
5 14 Israel Michiner married to Sarah Pickering, Joseph's Daughter; Cephas Child married same day
5 15 Hannah Kirkbride married to Samuel Estburn
5 22 Rachel Child was married to one Adkinson
5 14 Cephas Child married to widow Kenady they say
6 2 Thomas Dyer Esqr bought the Land of Josiah Dyer decd at a Sheriff's Sale for 400£
6 11 Sarah Wrights home bringing and her Daughter born the same Evening--
7 2 Hette Rich Died of a flux this morning about 1:00
7 11 Edward Moore's Child Died of a flux this evening, Bothers and Lions children Died within a few Days
7 30 Col Robert Robinson Drowned himself
8 3 William Doyls wife Died of a flux about 9:00 this morning
8-6 Barnet Hillyard's Child Died of a flux
8 12 Tarrants Monday married to Catte Lyon
8 17 Thos Good's son Died of a flux last night
8 24 Sarah Day Died of a flux
8 29 Joseph Thomas's son Mathew Died of a flux last night
9 4 William Preston's son Died Last night of a flux
9 7 Joseph Thomases son John Died of a flux
9 26 at night Joseph Shepards Daughter Born
11 5 William Davison Died this morning of a fever
11 7 Samuel Dyer from Susex was here & went to Philadelphia
11 26 Nanne Jones Buryed this day at the falls.
12-1 Nancy Moore & Polton set for MD
12-6 Bradshaw set off for MD but turned back

1789

1-6 Mary Good Died of Palsey
1 8 Joseph Wright moved to the Crooked Billit
1 2 Edward Moore's son born about 10:00 in the morning
1 2 Thomas Dyer, son of John & Jemima Dyer's of plumstead was born about 10:00 in the Evening 22 Jan.
4-7 Jude Morton moved from this town
4-7 Coombs moved here to Doyls Lott
Jo---Shepard moved to Day's old place---
4-16 Jose Rich & Eliz. Carlile married
4 16 Aaron Beans married to pol Burges
4 16 William Burges married to Doan

5-20 William Skelton moved to this town
6 11 David Stackhouse married to Michiner
6 22 Andrew Bray of NJ struck Dead by Lightening
6 22 John Cutler & his family set off for Niagary
6-23 John Furnesses Daughter born
7 3 Peter Woods Daughter born
7 15 Benjamin Kinsey buryed this Day
7 24 Daniel Carlile's Son's thigh bone broke---
8 1 George Bennets Daughter struck Dead by Lightning this Evening---
9 12 John Harts Wife Died of a feaver about 3:00 this morning
12 2 James Dyer from Susex came here

1790

1 5 Joseph Wright moved for Sussex Co, NJ G medows---
1 12 Alexander Shaw Departed this Life about 8:00 Last Night of a palsey, being as well as Common the 9th in the afternoon
1 12 Weasnor attorney at Law at Newtown Died the same Evening
1 13 Suffiah Stuart Died
1 30 Robert Walkers wife Died of a palsey this evening---
1 31 Sarah Jesop Died Last night of a Lingering disorder or old age (she was formerly widow of John Rich)
3-7 David Stackhouse's son born this Day
3 11 Jose Rich moved to El. Fentons
Jose Riches Daughter born
4 13 David Stackhouse moved from F.W.
4 13 Peter Wood moved from browns old Tavern & Willson & Brown moved to it
4-21 Andrew Ellicott moved to pettits Mill
4-26 Joseph Doan moved to John brown's John Brown moved him in the presents of Thomas Polton Jonathan Combs
5 24 Jonathan Shaw Departed this Life about 2:00 of a short Illness I believe a feavour
5 26 and was Buryed the 26th a very valuable member of Society I think
5-26 Corner Stones set By order of Doctor Joseph Watson Oliver Paxton & Isaac Hicks Arbitrators appointed by John Brown & Eleazor fenton on one part & John Dyer of the other part, Set by Isaac Hicks in the presents of Jacob Bennet Esqr. Sheriff & Jonathan Coombs & 3 sons
6-1 Jonathan Brown & his family moved over the blue Mountain
7 2 Phebe Moore Came here from Baltimore with her family
7 22 Mary Fenton Died about 3:00
7-30 Phebe Moores Daughter went to town to Live with Deborah Morris---
8 14 Mary Shaw died Last night of a Dropsey

10 21 William Doyl married to Rachel Fetherby

10-22 N. Brittain & J. Brittain moved to VA

11 1 John McCalla and family, Robert Shannon and family, moved for Sunsbury or Shamokin

11 25 Overbolt moved to Jonthan Browns old place
Abraham's son Lately married

11 23 Jonathan Doyl married to poly Stevens

1791

1 7 Aunt Ann Brown Departed this Life about 3 or 4 o'clock this morning

2-5 John Jones married to Betsy Preston

2-17 Edward Moores Daughter born this Day

2 19 Wm. Doyl Daughter born this morning

3 30 Chapman moved to his place Browns tavern

4 2 Jones child born

4-6 Jonathan Carlile moved from his place

4-7 John Bradshaw moved to F. Wrights

4-7 Jonathan Wells moved to Carliles place

4 11 Mathias Brown moved to Dilworths tavern

4 12 Joshua Walton moved for Chester Co

4-12 Isaac Willson moved to plains in plumstead

4-18 Edward Moore moved to D. Road

4 18 Joseph Shepard moved to F.D. place

4-28 Widdow Smith from near Ellicott's Mill moved for VA---

5-1 Jemima Dyer was delivered of a Daughter by Dr Meredith about 4:00 in the Afternoon & it was buryed the next day

5 20 Sally Wright and Nancy Moore set off for Sussex

6 9 Col Arthur Erwin was shot through and Died instantly in the house at tioga in the night or Evening and was brought down to tinicum and buryed the 17th

6-22 Thomas Dyer Esqr and Thomas Wright Contracted with Government for clearing the Lehigh from the falls to Easton for £1,000

7 9 Jane ottersons son born Died in about three days

7 20 John Bradshaws Daughter died last night (Rachel was her name)

9 5 Thomas Good died, an old man 90 odd years of age

10 8 John peningtons wife Died last night of a fevour---

11 20 George Erkinswallow to be buryed tomorrow at 10:00

11 20 And Minister James Greer of Deep Run at 12:00 tomorrow

11 21 W. Skelton, Miller moved from this town

11 22 Charles Stuart moved to Doyltown tavern Saml Flacks

11 23 Nathan Crook, Miller moved to this town

12-8 Joseph Wright & Salle here from Sussex with Elijah Collins and others

12-26 George Shaws son born Last night

1792
1 3 Levina Brown married to Amos Chapman
1 5 Jonathan Rich married to James Snodgrasses Daughter I hear
2-13 Joseph Pickering Died I believe
2-20 John Carey died I believe an old man, and was buryed this Day at
2-22 plumstead
Joseph Thomas Commissioned a few weeks ago---
3 20 Charles Stuarts Daughter married to Enoch Harvey at Doyl Town
3-22 Isaiah Michiner and Peggy Shepard married at Plumstead
3 28 Thomas Dyer set off for Wyoming and Swamp to build a sawmill for Wrights
4 2 John Jones Jur moved to horsham
4-3 Charles Stuart moved from Doyltown
4 3 John Shaw moved to Doyltown tavern that he bought of Saml Flack
4-3 Return Temple moved to John Brown's
4-3 John Bierly moved to John Jonese place---
4-9 Matthias Brown moved to his place
4-9 Barton Stuart wheelwright moved to Doyltown
4-10 Amos Chapman moved now abouts
10 Captain Greer moved to the Red Lion
4-10 Jane Greer married to Ralston---
4-10 Doctor Hugh Meredith moved to Doyltown within a few Days---
4 11 Matthias Brown Died about 4:00 of a short illness I believe---
4-12 John Furness moved from this town to a place of Benjamin Jamese's Down the Run
4-12 Jonathan Fell married to Townsend at Deep run (the weavers son)
4-13 Matthias Brown buryed at plumstead
4 16 William Walton moved for Chester Co this Day & Paul Preston moves to Andrew Ellicotts old place
4-20 Jonathan Hill here from paulinskill Susex Co, NJ---
5 11 Josiah Brown's son born---
5 16 Shoemaker moved to I Browns house---
5 25 Combes son born
6 21 a son of John Matthias's about 18 years of age killed by a tree
6 30 Rachel Dyer Daughter of John & Jemima Dyer's of plusmtead was born about 4:00 this morning (30 Jun 1792)
8 1 Jane otterson Died this morning about 6:00 (in this town)
8 28 polly Moore went to Live with Sally Ellicott in Philadelphia
9 1 Crooks son born this morning
9 2 Levina Chapmans Daughter born Last night I understand
9 5 James Shaw married to Widow Haring---

9-8 Mathew Grier Died last night or yesterday
9 11 Ephraim Shaw married the next day after his Father to Bradshaw
9 15 The Widdow Watson to be buryed tomorrow at 9:00 Thos' widow
9 27 Hette began the tayleress trade---
10 2 Ruth Poltons Daughter born last night
10 8 Edward Moore's Daughter born
10-9 Robert Kenedy married to Jane McCalla they say
10-11 Moses Wells married to Betsy Stuart this at George Stuarts
11-5 Action Entered against Jonathan Wells & John Rich at Nov term at Newtown

1793
1 1 Capt. Robert Thom Died now abouts
Salle Polton married to Jonathan Dunlap---
2 25 John Farris had a son born last night---
2 25 William Chapman Esqr's mother died this Day
3 16 John Bradshaw bought Titus Fells old place at a sheriffs sale about 970£
4-4 Joseph Rich moved to the falls
John Shaw moved to Fentons
4 4 Robert Kenedy moved near Schoolkills to a tavern he bought
4-9 John Robeson moved to this town---
4-10 Joseph Burges moved to this town to Furnesses Lot that he bought---
4-11 Patty Price Died this morning
4-11 John Faris moved this Day---
4-17 Jonathan Combs moved over the Run
4-21 Sally Shaw married to Eleazer Jones I understand
5 2 James Dunlap Likely to marry Guli Shewell
5 8 Wm. Plumer and Thomas Stackhouse here from Northampton
5 16 George Burges married to Rachel Carlile at plumstead this Day
5 16 James Dunlap married this Day
5 30 polly Shepard married to Masech Michiner
6 9 David Gilberts son drowned in Larges pond (so called)
7 1 Daniel Carlile's son Died this morning (very suddenly as he was well yesterday) soposed by Drinking of Spirits threw him into fits
7 24 Edward Moores son John Died this afternoon of a flux
7 27 John Penington married to Peggy Edwards they say
8 13 My Aged Mother in Law Departed this Life 13 Aug about 11:00 at Night of a flux & plurycy I believe
8 14 Sarah Dyer Wife of Thos Dyer Esqr Departed this Life (of a plurecy) 14 Aug at Night late near 12:00 or influensey
8 15 Sarah Moore was buryed in the forenoon and Sarah Dyer in the afternoon at Plumstead

8 17 Searls Shewells Wife died this morning

9 2 John Willson says that about ¼ of the people has Left town on account of the sickness and that about 50 a Day has Died for 10 Days past---

9 12 Moses Rich Departed this Life between 10 & 11 o'clock 12 Sep 1793.

10-3 Francis Goods two daughters Died in Philadelphia within a few Days we hear

10-10 John Meredith Doctor, died last night of the Disorder or distemper---

10-11 polly Michiner or Shepard's daughter born

11 11 My Sister Phebe Moore Departed this Life 11 Nov about Sun set 1793 of a consumption I believe after a lingering painfull Illness, She Departed this life very Quietly

11 13 My beloved Sister was buryed 13 Nov 1793 at plumstead
Rachel Brown came from the mountain to see her about two days before her Departure & staid the burial

11 21 Daniel Evans Departed this Life---

11 23 Joseph Moore went to live at James Shaws son of Phebe Moore decd

11 24 Recd some account of the Death of my Brother Joseph Dyer about three weeks a Go from this Day by John Townsend who came from MD I understand this Day---

12 12 Polly Moore went to live with Joseph Riches

1794

1 6 Gaberil Swartslander's son Died of the small pox I believe---

2 3 John Large perished in the snow near his own house Last night and Joseph Terry was near perishing in billy Beals medow I understand and in the Day Wm Preston was hurt be the stove pipe at Buckinham meeting

2 6 Nancy Moore moved to Thos Dyers this day---

2-10 Donte Browns child born I understand

2 15 Josiah Browns child Died
Jonathan Browns Junr child born the 10th of this month

2-23 Daniel Burges buryed this day

2 24 John Robeson Died this afternoon in this town (about 6:00)

3 8 Nancy More a Son born this morning about 2:00 (Barton Stuart)

3 15 Sally Jones Daughter born Last night

3 17 John Bradshaw moved to Zenas Fells old place, same day Amos Bradshaw moved to this town

3-20 Salle Jones Departed this Life last night about 12:00, and was

3 21 buryed this Day

3-22 Nancy Combs's daughter born this morning about 3:00

3-24 James Moore went to live with John Burges to learn the weaver trade

3 31 Abraham Brown moved for Chester Co this morning

3 31 Isaac Willson moved for Chester this day, and Wm. Townsend also---

4 3 Zenas Fell moved to this town
4 4 Amos Bradshaw's Daughter born last night
4 7 Mahlon Michiner moved for Chester Co this morning
4 7 Widdow Robeson moved for North wales from this town
4-7 Wm Nicholas moved to this town
4 15 Thos Good moved for Chester Co
5 15 Zenas Fells son Zenas Died of the Small pox this evening---
5-18 burial of Joseph Gillingham (son of John) this afternoon who Died of a consumption---
5 23 the widow of John Carey died this day or Last night I believe---
6 9 Martha Furness died Last night
7 13 Patrick poe Died suddenly
8 3 Isaac Martin from Rahway had a meeting at Kirkbrides this afternoon
8 18 Martin Scott buryed this Day
8 18 Peter Cosmer moved his family to Chester Co, Londonderry township
9 6 The militia of PA & also the militia of the other States called to Go against the Redstone boys so called, being the Inhabitants on the west side of the Allegany mountains in PA & VA Who Refuse to pay the Still Duty
10 6 Benjamin Days son born last nig about
10-14 the general election of seven townships in one District held at Wm Chapmans
10 14 John Furnes married this evening
10 23 Wm Nicholas moved from this town
12 1 Joseph Coulter moved to Nicholas house
12 14 John Carey Departed this Life about 8:00 this morning of a lingering Decay for some months
12 15 account Recd of John Ellicott's Death (in MD)
12 21 Joseph Burges'es Son born (Jonathan)
12 22 Cephas Childs'es wife died last night

1795
1 2 Martha Fenton Departed this Life last night at 11:00
1 17 Recd a Recommendation, Jona Brown
1 21 John Rich married to Mary, Wm Prestons daughter, they say
1 24 John Kallender was run over by his wagon at or near Philadelphia the 20th of this month & so bruised that he died the next morning
1 28 Jacob Overholt's daughter born
2-13 John Moore bound by Thos Wright his uncle for four years & one month to Wm Ashby to learn the tailors trade in Philadelphia

2-15 John Penn one of the family of the former proprietors of penn Silvania, was buryed at Christ Church 12 Feb 1796, Philadelphia, Grandson to William Penn the first founder of PA & the City of Philadelphia.

2-16 Aaron Shaw went apprentice to Oliver Hampton wheel maker & turner

2 19 Patty Rich married to Dave Worthington (they say)
John Baracreft died about the 16th of this month of a pluerecy

2-25 George Shaws son born last night

3 1 polly moore went to James Shaw to live

3 4 Wm Heaton Died Last night, formerly Inn keeper at Red Lion I understand. He died near Jenkintown of a pluricy.

3 26 Jonas Doan married to Permela Price; and Jacob Paringer married to Kaziah Harding at Esqr Hughes'es

4-4 Samuel Fenton's wife to be buryed tomorrow at 9:00

4-5 the Widdow Percilla Gilbert to be buryed tomorrow at 9:00---

4 6 Jonathan Wells moved for Chester Co with Walton

4-7 the next day Skelton moved from Fentons mill to J. Browns old house where Job lived
Worthington moved to Fentons

4-8 Eleanor Carey moved to her place
Kirk moved to Wm Beals place---

4-12 Josiah Browns son born

4-14 John Shaw moved for Chester Co

4-16 Edward Moore moved to John Shaws old place this day

4-22 Wm Beal moved his family to VA

4-26 Nathan Crook's son born this morning

4-27 John Faris moved for VA

5 6 a Grandson of John Burroughs of the name of Isaac Thornton was hurt by a fall from a horse so that he died in a short time

5-13 Smith Price married to Hannah Jones at his house

6 4 Saml Gilbert married to Hulda Jones

6 13 Richard Beckhouse (Late assistant Judge) died suddenly in Philadelphia

7 8 Mary Preston Departed this Life between 10 & 11 o'clock Last night of a Lingering of two or three years

7 23 Thos West buryed this day

8 13 John Riches son born last night

9 3 Joseph Shepards daughter born Last night I think

9 6 John Peningtons daughter born last night

9 10 Jonathan Rich'es son born this evening

9 17 Gainer Good married to Charles Hutchin

10-10 John Fell Departed this Life last evening of a lingering disease & is to be buryed the 11th at 9:00

10 16 William Doyl's daughter born

10 22 Ludwick Switzer Menonest Minister died last night I believe
10 28 John Riches home bringing
11 3 Wm Bradshaws Daughter married to Joseph Johnson at plumstead this day
11 12 Joseph Shaw married to Tyson at Jenkintown this Day I under stand
11 16 Sally Dyer own Daughter went to Joseph Burges'es to learn the weaver trade if her Constitution be strong enough to bear it
11 18 John Worthington's child died at other mill
11-20 Josiah Coulters daughter born 11:00
11 28 Joseph Michiners wife Died near Germantown
12-15 Doctor Meredith's daughter married to A. Chapman attorney

1796
1 3 Dave Worthingtons son born last night
1 3 Susannah Smith died Last night at Saml Gilberts I understand of a short illness of about 4 days
1 22 Smith Prices son (by second wife Hannah Jones) born this Day
1 24 Salley Budd, Francis Goods granddaughter Died this afternoon
1 29 Daniel Stradling Departed this Life this morning of a lingering decay with age
1 29 Levina Chapmans daughter born
2-1 Robert Kirkbride Junr went to MD to Ellicotts mills to tend store for one year
2 3 Nathaniel Shewel married to Cinthy Fell at Esqr Rodmans this evening
2 19 Hulda Gilberts son born last night, formerly Hulda Jones, married Sam Gilbert
2-28 Roiley's wife buryed
3 6 Mary Harvey buried this Day she died of a pluresy I hear a sister of John Brown
3 12 Tommey Wright went to Philadelphia to tend store at Jesse Sharplesses
3 18 Josiah Wright started for Wilksbarre with a view of seting up the printing office for a news paper at that place
3 20 paddy Fenton married I hear
3 27 Mary Wells left her husband last fall and Wm Preston set off with her this morning to see if he would use her better to try to reconcile them
3 27 Capt. John Jemison buryed this day
3 29 Amos Chapman moved for Chester Co about 3:00 this morning with his family
4-6 Ashur Foulk moved to McCallas old place---
4-6 John Rich moved to Wm Prestons place
4 6 Saml Fell moved to Chapmans
4 6 Silas Preston married to Francis Goods daughter

4-6 Plumleys moving to Esqr Rodmans from Jersey I understand
4-7 Benjamin fell married ----- Jean –
4 12 Francis Good & family moved for Chester Co
4-14 Nathan Crook miller left the mill very suddenly or without giving satisfaction
4-14 Thomas Poulton & Amos Bradshaw moved Nathan Crook from my house---
4 14 Jonathan Combs took possession of the mill before the expiration of the Leas
6 10 John Moore died about 7:00 this morning after having fits for 40 years or more, from the age of 22 years which had reduced him to a Child like state. He was buryed at plumstead.
6-18 Samuel Fenton Died about 10:00
6-16 Eleazor Fenton married to the widow Brown, at Esqr Hughes'es they say
6-17 Sally Dyer left Burges from learning the weaver trade---
7 2 Hannah Shaw married to Eleazor Jones---
7-6 Nathaniel Ellicott Died this afternoon or evening of a short Illness---
7 10 Widdow Erkinswallow hanged herself
7 13 Nathan Doan moved to this town his wife was Rachel Evans---
8 24 Thomas Lewis to be buryed tomorrow at 10:00 I hear---
8 29 Eleazer Jones moves to Pownals
9 12 Jose Wright and Robt Kirkbride Junr started for wilksbarre to enter into partnership
9 15 I hear that James Job & his wife was struck Dead in the Jersey last night
9 28 Hugh Merns killed with his mill I understand on Nashamany
10 13 Joseph Watson buryed this day at Buckingham, a worthy man---
11 2 Ure Bradfield died about noon of an Influanseycal disorder. She was a very fat woman.
11 11 Robert Skelton buryed who died of a Dropsey after a Long illness
11 21 Ephraim Evans & wife here from Red stone, where they moved last Spring
12 1 Samuel Dean moved Wm Doyls lot
12 4 Benjamin Scott to be buryed tomorrow
12 11 I hear that Isaiah Rich died 22 Nov---
12-16 Elizabeth Dyer 2nd daughter of John and Jemima Dyers of plumstead was born 15 Dec about 11:00 1796
12 15 David Kirkbride married to polly Jones, at Strawns tavern---
12 22 Ambros poulton married to Eliza White---
12-27 Nancy Moore moved to Joseph Riches

1797

1 11 My aged father in law Departed this Life about 1:00 on 11 Jan 1797 about 89 years.

1 26 Abraham Chapman married they say to ----- Fell at Esqr Bursons 26 Jan.

1 28 Jane Thomas an old welch woman of good Character I believe Died this day of old age in some measure---

1-30 Jonathan Combs'es son Thomas Died last night about 8:00 of a Short illness

2-6 Joseph Thomases wife Died last night of a kind of Lunacy I hear---

2 7 John Riche's wife had 2 Daughters born Last night---

2-9 Jonathan Kinsey Died last night

2 12 Israel Doan buryed at plumstead, a very antiant man near 100 years old I hear

3-4 The president of the united states takes his seat this day, the second Adams from Newengland who had been vice president under Washington who Resigned the office

3 23 Mathew Greer Jur married to Salle Snodgrass

4-3 Esther Dyer passed meeting with John Michiner---

4-4 Samuel Fell moved to Kinseytown

4-4 Cadwalader Foulk moved to Swamp---

4-4 Funk to F. Goods old place

4 7 Joseph Coulter moved from this Town to Esqr Ingham's place

4-8 Thomas Good from Chester Co

4 10 George Shaw moved from his place that he sold to J. Fell

4-11 Abraham Chapman that married Saml Fell's daughter moved for Chester Co

4-22 Polly wells went home to Chester Co

4 25 Lisias Blakes married to pownal---

5 18 Esther Dyer daughter of John & Jemima Dyer's of plumstead was married to John Michiner

5 30 Esther Late Dyer moved from this town to Joseph Watkins's near Ellicotts mill in plumstead 30 May 1797

6 8 Elizabeth Paxson (formerly Brown) Died last night of a lingering Consumption---

6 9 Widdow Paxson died, Fells Daughter

6 9 I was at the burial of Elizabeth Paxson

6 15 David Kirkbride's daughter born this morning and paddy fentons Daughter born the same day I hear

7-4 Nathaniel Shewels son born last night

7-4 Robert Shelel died at S. Deans of a Consumption, Cousen to N. Shewell of Doyltown, Esqr Shewles brothers son

7-6 Jonathan Shepard married to Jemima Large his housekeeper

7 23 Alexander Brown son of John at plumstead

8 4 James Dyer came from Wilksbarre
9 2 Ure Blankinhom Died
9 2 Smith prices Son born I hear
9 4 George Shaw moved for Chester Co
9 6 Joseph Burges's son born
10 4 Jane Beaumont Died last night of a consumption
10 8 Patty Worthington formerly Rich Died Last night I hear---
10 10 Eli Worthington fell from a horse & the horse fell on him so that he Died in about 3 days
10 12 Sarah Church an old woman buried this day
10 16 Hannah Shaws Daughter born
10 24 Nathan Doan moved from this town for Berwick over Susquehannah between Sunbury & Wilksbarre Northumberland Co
10 28 Samuel Deans Daughter born last night; Partners son buryed and Carver buryed, Smith prices first father in law, I hear
10 30 Ambros poulton a Daughter born
10 28 Abraham Chapmans wife (Millisan) died in Childbed & was buryed this day
11 20 John Brown Departed this Life this morning about 8:00
11 21 Nancy Moore moved to Riches
11 23 John Michiner moved to Amos Allbrites place that he bought this fall
12-7 Joseph Shepards son born last night I understand
12-16 Jonathan Shepards son born last night I understand—

1798
1 16 James Dunlap moved to the store at the Red Lion or Willowgrove
1 17 A dreadful accident happened at John Crutz's one Jacob Ruth a carpenter felling a tree, the tree not falling as expected the but of it fell on his breast & he died instantly (had a wife & 4 or 5 children)
1 22 Smith Prices son John Price married to Betsy Kirk at Esqr Bursons
2 15 Letitia Kirkbride married to Jonathan Good at plumstead
2021 Peter Yarnall of bybery Died of a plursey I hear, an Excelant Inspired minister of the Gospel tis thought
2-27 Henry Kirkes Died at night of a bilious Cholic I hear
3 15 John Shaw married to Patty Brown at plumstead
3 15 Ulisus Blaker moved to this town at 3£ per annum
3 20 Esther Michiner's (formerly Dyer) son born between 1 & 2 o'clock in the morning of 25 Mar 1798 Absolem
3 28 John Michner Died this morning, Grandfather to our Son in law
4-3 Moses Dunlap moved to Wm Chapman's place by Kirks as Chapman's family moves bit by bit, or Stranely to DE Co about 10 miles from Philadelphia

4-5 Amos Bradshaw moved to DE Co from this town, Wrights place
4-5 John vanforson moved to T. Wrights place in this town
4-5 Esqr Hughes son married to Jane McFaggin at the billit
4 5 Aaron Maulsberry moved to I. Worthingtons house
4-9 Charles plumly moved for Chester Co
4 9 Stephen Moore moved from Jersey to James Shaw's place
4-12 James Faris moved to Dente Browns place
4-29 William Preston's wife Died last night after a long & Lingering Illness
5 22 Alexander Hughs Esqr Died this afternoon of a fevour I hear
5 24 Josiah Wright arrived from wilksbarre this eveing with Esqr Dyer & W. Taylor Recd letters by them from the surveying Company, G. Burges, A. Brown, R. Kirkbride, C. Fell, I. Moore, I. Matlen, I. Craig, W. Loyd Wm Robins, F. Wright, John Dyer
5 27 Esqr Shewell's house burned
5-28 yesterday morning Ulisus Blaker's son Samuel Born in this town
6 15 Betty Brown married to preston
7 29 Joseph Moore went to live at Ambrose Poultons
7-23 Nancy Moore brought her Brother Joseph Moore from James Shaws
7-31 Samuel Gillingham Comisr began an arch bridge over this Creek
8-16 Philip Moore Junr moved to my house
8 27 John Bradfield Died this evening about 7:00 of a fevour
9 30 Wm Hills son born this day
10 1 Robert Kirkbride Died last night of the yallow fevour & was buryed this forenoon
10 5 Anna Kirkbride a blooming youth died this forenoon & was buryed this afternoon of the fevour
10 18 Josiah Rich married to Patty Preston I hear---
10-25 Ambros Poulton a son born last night
10 25 Israel vanluvans married to Rachel Burns (Elen Caryes girl)
10 31 John Fells son born
11 8 John Robeson married to Deborah Kerr at Esqr Walls---
10 14 Alexr Shaw married to pate willson
12-6 George Stewart moved to Doyltown this day---
12 10 Letitia Goods Daughter born—

1799

1-2 David Kirkbrides Daughter born this morning
1-4 Isaac Hill buried this day, died of cancer in the throat---
1-4 Isaac Pickering buryed this day I understand, at buckingham
1 8 The first assessment for house & window tax in America
1-18 Stephen Moores son born Last night I understand
1 25 Thomas Ellicott Died of a pluricy or fevour---

1 28 Josiah Brown's son born

2-7 Jonathan Child married to D. Michiner

2-11 John Krotz's wife Died this evening of a bilious Cholick or lingering disease unknown

2-13 Jonathan Ingham formerly Esqr an antiant man (of his time a wise majestrate) was buryed this day I understand---

2-27 Josiah Riches Wife delivered of two daughters this morning

3 14 Josiah Shaw an old Setler in plumstead Departed this Life last night about 8:00, not long poorlyer than common as I have heard of, but age

3 19 Jonathan Riches son born

3 21 Smith Prices son born---

3 27 Jude Morton Died about this day I understand

4-16 Alexander Matlen Died last night, I hear Thomas Dyer very poorly, I wrote to Wilksbarre to his friends

4-20 John Morison buryed this day

4 20 Wm Bradshaws son, several accidential or suden Deaths I hear

4-24 Hanah Burges died last night after a very short Illness

6 14 John Gillingham's wife buryed, died of Consumption

6-19 Hugh Farguson Died last night an old settler in plumstead as any now left I believe---

7-5 Brother Thomas Dyer formerly Esqr Departed this life between 1 & 2 o'clock last night or this morning of a Lingering consumptive Complaint, 27 Mar came here & kept his bed for nearly 3 months first began with a bilious fevour and after that to a Decay or Consumption which wasted his flesh & brought him so Low that he could scarcely speak, was buried the 6th at plumstead

7-11 John Shaw's son born last night I hear

7 13 John Thompson, miller, buryed

7 26 Thos Jones of buckingham Died this morning

8 15 David Gilbert died last night of an appoplex I hear

10-15 Abraham Brown Jr died last night of a Cholick or short illness

10-9 John Moore (Father of Edward Moore now of plumstead) Died about 11:00 this day of a long and Lingering decay of 6 months or more

10 15 Abraham Brown son of Abm Brown died of a very short Illness soposed a kind of Cholick or bilious feavour, he came from Baltimore a few weeks ago as the people there were very sickly

10 17 John Robeson's daughter born last night, David Carrs son in law---

10 18 Alexander Shaw's daughter born last night

10 20 Amos Shaw died about 10:00

Our Jonne came home from the Federal City, Alexandria, Georgetown & Baltimore Last night, the greatest abuses ever I knew Electionearing before & at the General Election

10-22 Susanah Combs son born this morning said to be Amos Merricks
10-26 Levina Chapman starts home for Chester Co with Charles Fell & little Titus
10 29 Richard Meredith died of a very short illness of fits or yallow fevour at Wm Merediths
11 7 Polly Shaw's daughter born last night
Jonne Beaumont, Sally Willson from Chester Co here
12 16 Jonathan Childs first son born last night
12 20 Jonathan Shepards Child died last night
12-21 Philip Moores son born about 4:00 this afternoon
Lieutenant General George Washington of Mount Vernon in VA Departed this Life 14 Dec 1799 in the evening of Quinsey in 23 hours Illness
12-28 Ulisus Blake's daughter born this morning
12 29 Salle Moore married to Jesse Jones at Aaron Warfords

1800
1 1 Jonne Came from wilksbarre after purchasing Wrights place £1300 for 117 acres and his goods Left
1 2 Salle Hartly married to Jo Scarborough
1 14 Jesse Dyer left here the 7th of this month to Choose a guardian proposed to Choose William Preston Cause me some trouble as I had subscribed to Thos Gibson for him to go to school and did not hear of his going Away, tho, I believe it was from bad Councilers caused Jesse to dispise the Council of his best friends
1 19 Josiah Poulton married to Polly Moore at Esqr Burson's
2 3 Jesse Dyer Chose Wm Preston for his Guardian this day I hear---
2-7 Philip Moore move to philadelphia
3-18 Josiah Wright married
4 1 Vanfossen moved from wrights old place to Shoemaker Town or near it
4-1 Ulisus Blaker moved to wrights place---
4-1 Jonathan Child moved to same place---
4 3 Stephen Large moved from Fenton's mill, near Shoemaker town
4 8 Joseph Shepards son born this morning
4-8 Josiah Poulton moved to this town
5-5 Nathan Price Departed this Life, an old Setler in these parts & father of Smith Price of plumstead
5-7 Isaac Walton died last night
Joseph Kinsey buryed this day
5-15 Ulisus Blakers son died last night
5 16 Widdow Perry died this morning
5 29 ----- Crout buryed this day, Died of a bilious feavour

6 15 Josiah Wright came from Camp with the Discharge from Military Service, a Discharge of the army took place
6 24 Francis Good of Chester Co killed by his wagon forcing him against a tree while he was taking it down a hill
8 6 John Michiner & Esther had a son born this morning about 8:00
8 10 Salle Wright came from Wilkesbarre with Letitia her daughter
8 28 Zenas Fell moved for Niagarre
8 28 Mary Wright with Josiah's wife & Caleb Wrights wife and Children with T. Wright Jur here from Wilksbarre
9 2 Joseph Burges'es son born this evening about 9:00
9 11 Hannah Burges married to Thomas Roberts at plumstead
9 11 Ephraim Jones married to Phebe Price in Jersey
9 29 David Kirkbrides son born last night I believe---
10 11 T. Wright Jur left philadelphia
10 17 Jesse Jones's son born last night (formerly Salle Moore)
10 23 John Fells daughter born I hear
10 26 William Doyl Departed this Life about 8:00 this morning of a swelling on his breast or throat, an old Inhabitant of this Neighborhood aged 88 years lived in Doyltown & this town most of the time---
11-13 Moses Quinby married to Hannah Good at plumstead
1801
1 7 Polly Poultons son born about 9:00 this eveing; formerly polly moore
1 15 Samuel Gillinghams new mill began to Grind about this time
1 29 William Preston using all his endeavours to overthrow the settlement of the Estate of Thos Dyer decd & causeing it to be sported away at law in a very Disagreeable manner, to the disadvantage of the dear orphans takes evidences, Thomas Poulton, Jonathan Combs, John Bradshaw & John Moore this adjourned orphans Court; and ever since he was so fortunate as to be chosen guardian has been very full of Deception to the executor persuadeing him that it was not necessary to make a settlement in the year, till a final settlement could be made and immediately put in a petition to the Court to have him Removed & had actually applied to a person to Except of that trust but failed as yet, but now is to make a grand push with his number of evidences
1 29 David Forst buryed this day I hear
1 29 Sarah Stradling widow of Daniel Stradling late of plumstead died this day
2 1 Samuel Armitage an old man buried this day
2 7 Joseph Fell (of Doyltown) died this morning of a bilious cholic---
2-10 Smith Price's daughter born last night, his first Daughter---
2-10 John Smith's wife died this day
2-11 John Dyer Jur married I believe

2 17 My sister in law Rhoda Moore died this morning of a Lingering Consumption of about 12 months

3 8 John Wigton buryed this day, an old settler aged about 100 years---

3-18 Benjamin Stephen's wife buryed this day

3 28 Jonathan Childs'es son born last night

3-28 Josiah Poultons son Jesse an infant was found dead in the bed this morning---

3 31 Josiah Poulton moved from this town

3 31 Aaron Maulsbery moved to this town this day at 4£ per annum

4-6 Rachel Brown widow of John Brown decd & formerly widow of Isaac Child died last night of a very violent disorder in her sences and fits

4-10 David Cummings of willow grove buried at Horsham this day---

4-15 John Shaw's son born last night

4 20 Esqr Coffmans daughter born last night

4-23 Cornelious Shepard married

4-27 Alexr Shaw's daughter born last night

5 1 James Shaw departed this Life last night or evening, after a tedious & Lingering decay or Rhumatic complaint of more than 12 months, Being the last of the old stock of Shaws, and was bured at

5 2 plumstead this day

5-4 Tommy Wright started for Wilkesbarre as he had left printing some time

5-5 Bekkey Stiner married last night to David Swager I hear

6 1 Isaac Miers buryed this day had been consumpted for 4 or 5 months kept his bed

6-10 Asher Miner T. Wrights son in law from Wilkesbarre very earnest for pollys Legacy before he returns

6-30 John Prices son born last night

7 8 John poulton married to foster I hear

7 11 Morris Morris'es wife Died about 11:00 this day

8-10 the flux very mortal about Durham & Springfield, I. Brock buryed three Children & I hear of 11 burials in a day

8 26 Isaac Thomas's son died of a flux

8 27 Israel Monroe moved to Esqr old house this day

8 27 Wm Bryon's child died of a flux

9 1 Jonathan Worthington died Last night or this morning early---

9 17 Jacob Dintsman's Child died of a flux

PRESBYTERIAN CHURCH, CHURCHVILLE

Originally published in the *Pennsylvania Archives*, Volume 9, 2nd Series.

25 Nov 1738	Adams, Susanna and Hendrick Roos
6 Mar 1771	Addis, Martha and Joseph Harding
11 Mar 1772	Akee, Joseph and Leena Bennet
27 May 1762	Anderson, Nancy and Henry Jones
16 Dec 1765	Anderson, Sarah and Joseph Murdock
18 Jul 1753	Anderson, William and Elizabeth McInsley
21 Sep 1749	Arsen, Matthew and Elizabeth Strickler
31 Dec 1746	Ashton, Deborah, and William Waters
16 Nov 1772	Baldertson, Josiah and Martha Ely
4 Apr 1763	Baldwin, John and Massey Sotcher
23 Apr 1771	Barcroft, Ambrose and Phoebe Quimby
23 Apr 1771	Barcroft, Hannah and Edward Rise
27 May 1765	Barnes, Agnes and Abraham Foster
20 Apr 1769	Barnet, Margaret and Robert Sibbett
9 Jan 1809	Barns, Jacob and Mary Erwin
25 Apr 1769	Barr, Adam and Charity West
24 Jun 1804	Barrack, Mary and William Palmer
5 Dec 1745	Bartholomew, William and Maria Thomas
22 Oct 1761	Beckker, Maria and Hendrick Bexter
28 May 1765	Beebe, Sarah and William Roberson
23 Aug 1757	Bennet, Aart and Lena Knowles
11 Jun 1756	Bennet, Benjamin and Jannetye Van Sicklen
12 May 1757	Bennet, Elizabeth and Gerardus Wykoff
7 Dec 1758	Bennet, Elizabeth and Garret Wynkoop
17 Aug 1768	Bennet, Elizabeth and Henry Huddleston
16 Apr 1765	Bennet, Hendrick and Elizabeth White
17 Oct 1745	Bennet, Isaac and Maria Van Horn
14 Sep 1754	Bennet, Isaac and Margaritta Van Dyk
16 Sep 1804	Bennet, Isaac and Mary Corson
23 Dec 1761	Bennet, Jan and Annitye Jones
5 Mar 1789	Bennet, Jane and William Vanzant
23 Aug 1756	Bennet, Jannetye and Jacobus Vansant
13 Feb 1766	Bennet, Jannetye and Johannis Roberts
8 Apr 1742	Bennet, Johannis and Elizabeth Van Pelt
11 Dec 1746	Bennet, Johannis and Magdalen Bennet
12 Jan 1769	Bennet, Leah and Derrick Hogeland
11 Mar 1772	Bennet, Leena and Joseph Akee
24 Mar 1772	Bennet, Leentye and Abraham Van Horn
28 May 1800	Bennet, Lott and Mary Carroll

11 Dec 1746	Bennet, Magdalen and Johannis Bennet
16 Feb 1758	Bennet, Maria and Derrick Krusen
3 Nov 1801	Bennet, Mary and Joseph Randolph
18 Apr 1758	Bennet, Ryk. and Jannetye Sedam
21 Dec 1763	Bennet, Simson and Klartye Sackett
8 Nov 1801	Bennett, William and Mary Kroesen
10 Nov 1766	Betts, Maria and Samuel Headley
17 Nov 1799	Bewley, Jesse and Mary Fenton
22 Oct 1761	Bexter, Hendrick and Maria Beckker
7 Dec 1767	Bigelow, Esther and Joseph Henry
26 Jun 1766	Biles, William and Hannah Kirkbridge
19 Apr 1770	Blake, John and Catharine Stevens
7 Feb 1765	Bogaet, Susanna and Jores Nevins
27 Dec 1739	Bohm, Elizabeth and Jurick Juhambach
31 Dec 1741	Booskirk, Jannetye and Barent Van Hoorn
29 Jul 1742	Boskirk, Andries and Guertrie Van Hoorn
26 Dec 1789	Both, Hendrick and Marcillis Klenklin
12 Feb 1761	Brant, Jacob and Doortye Fisher
8 Jun 1769	Brees, Charity and Samuel Mitchell
22 Nov 1764	Brees, Elizabeth and John Hatton
30 Jan 1765	Brees, Elizabeth and Samuel Linten
15 Dec 1771	Brees, John and Susannah Cooper
17 Mar 1808	Bretsford, Jemima and Jabez Sevenst
6 Nov 1802	Briggs, Martha and Samuel Murray
11 Aug 1763	Britton, Sarah and Jesse Williamson
9 Jun 1763	Britton, Thomas and Sarah Harvey
16 Aug 1785	Bross, Esther and Benjamin Sweetser
11 Sep 1789	Brown, John and Eleanor Vanzant
12 May 1799	Brown, Leana and John Duffield
10 Mar 1768	Bulger, Thomas and Leah Harvey
4 Oct 1770	Burdsall, Sarah and William Pettir
26 May 1801	Burlay, Jane and Wm Turner
18 Oct 1742	Butcher, Johannis and Maria Swarks
27 Oct 1768	Butterworth, Thomas and Eleanor McNiss
27 Jan 1763	Campbell, Mary and John Grant
28 May 1800	Carroll, Mary and Lott Bennett
30 Dec 1760	Carter, William and Rebecca Sirl
25 Jan 1767	Carver, Elizabeth and Joseph Worthington
15 Apr 1747	Carvour, Ann and Robert Heaton
15 Apr 1747	Carvour, John and Rachel Naylor
11 Dec 1739	Cassidan, Marsilis and Hans Michael Thielsheven
13 Jan 1755	Cephard, Johan Wilhelm and Eva Catrina Hickman

5 Nov 1769	Chandler, Jane and James Welsh
23 Oct 1766	Clawson, William and Rachel Stout
13 Oct 1766	Comley, Joshua and Catharine Willet
15 Dec 1771	Cooper, Susannah and John Brels
25 Dec 1771	Corbit, Phoebe and John Dungan
16 Nov 1803	Cornell, Adrian and Eleanor Craven
2 Nov 1809	Cornell, Cornelia and Gillian Cornell
17 Nov 1803	Cornell, Cynthia and James Cornell
27 Oct 1799	Cornell, Elizabeth and Henry Feaster
2 Nov 1809	Cornell, Gillian and Cornelia Cornell
16 Nov 1809	Cornell, Gillian and Elizabeth Kroesen
17 Nov 1803	Cornell, James and Cynthia Cornell
5 Dec 1809	Cornell, James and Margaret Vandegrift
12 Jan 1809	Cornell, Margaret and Henry Feaster
28 May 1801	Cornell, Martha and Aaron Feaster
5 Nov 1760	Cornell, Simon and Adrienne Kroesen
14 Apr 1744	Cornel, Wilhelm and Essie Kroesen
11 Jan 1804	Cornell, William and Jane Craven
25 Nov 1810	Cornell, Wilhelmus and Anne Lefferts
1 Nov 1804	Cornely, Elizabeth and John Worthington
17 Oct 1742	Cornish, Thomas and Catharine Egberd
20 Mar 1799	Corson, Anna and Kasper Keyser
2 Jan 1741/2	Corson, Benjamin and Maria Sedam
16 Feb 1755	Corson, Cornelius and Margaritta Van Enden
14 Jun 1810	Corson, Jane and Henry Vanartsdalen
16 Sep 1804	Corson, Mary and Isaac Bennet
25 Jan 1810	Corson, Mary and Charles Finney
25 Jun 1809	Corson, Richard and Hannah Vanartsdalen
4 Nov 1801	Corsen, Wilhelmus and Mary Murray
27 Aug 1772	Craven, Cornelia and William Craven
16 Nov 1803	Craven, Eleanor and Adrian Cornell
6 Jan 1808	Craven, Elizabeth and Jesse Finney
11 Jan 1804	Craven, Jane and William Cornell
27 Aug 1772	Craven, William and Cornelia Craven
10 Jan 1771	Crozier, Ann and Hugh Morton
20 Jul 1763	Davis, Grace and David Terry
14 Oct 1772	Davis, Olly and Thomas Ferry
25 Jun 1768	Davis, Sarah and Henry Lewis
23 May 1800	Dean, John and Mary Paterson
23 Nov 1761	Derbyshire, John and Mary Rickey
19 Nov 1789	Dongan, Nelley and Leffert Lefferts
7 Mar 1763	Dooley, Sarah and Paul Pennington

19 Dec 1766	Doughty, Daniel and Martha Laning
5 Nov 1767	Doughty, Elizabeth and Abraham Lewis
20 Feb 1745/6	Drake, Jonathan and Martha Thomas
25 May 1795	DuBois, Helen and David Taggert
23 Dec 1804	Dubois, Helena and John Lefferts
18 Dec 1751	DuBois, Jonathan and Helletye Wynkoop
30 Nov 1742	Duffield, John and Martha Mattuck
12 May 1799	Duffield, John and Leanna Brown
31 Mar 1744	Dun, Roelf and Anna Heaton
25 Dec 1771	Dungan, John and Phoebe Corbit
25 Oct 1759	Dunn, Mary and George Randall
31 Mar 1763	Eastburn, Mary and Samuel Roberts
4 Jan 1798	Edwards, Jesse and Elizabeth Nobles
17 Oct 1742	Egberd, Catharine and Thomas Cornish
19 Aug 1804	Egbert, Lydia and Isaac Kroesen
16 Nov 1772	Ely, Martha and Josiah Baldertson
4 May 1758	Engard, Carrol and Maria Stevens
14 Nov 1742	Ernst, Baltus and Maria Pokinson
5 Apr 1810	Erwin, Cadwalader and Jane Jones
27 Oct 1767	Erwin, Jane and John Johnson
9 Jan 1809	Erwin, Mary and Jacob Barry
30 Dec 1799	Estee, John and Elizabeth McNeal
2 Jul 1807	Evans, Britain and Rachel Raine
28 May 1801	Feaster, Aaron and Martha Cornell
13 Sep 1768	Feaster, David and Maria Hageman
10 Mar 1808	Feaster, Elizabeth and Richd Fenton
27 Oct 1799	Feaster, Henry and Elizabeth Cornell
12 Jan 1809	Feaster, Henry and Margaret Cornell
13 Jan 1789	Feaster, Mary and William McCrum
1 Nov 1770	Feathers, Deborah and Samuel Titus
11 Jul 1799	Fenton, John and Elizabeth Johnson
25 May 1795	Fenton, Joseph and Mary Vanartsdalen
19 Aug 1804	Fenton, Joseph and Catharine Kroesen
21 Mar 1765	Fenton, Leentye and Garret Kroesen
7 Apr 1800	Fenton, Martha and John Smith
17 Nov 1799	Fenton, Mary and Jesse Bewley
25 May 1795	Fenton, Mary and John Vanartsdalen
6 Apr 1810	Fenton, Mary and Simon Lefferts
23 Aug 1770	Fenton, Matthias and Rachel Hardy
10 Mar 1808	Fenton, Richard and Elizabeth Feaster
11 Mar 1801	Ferron, John M. and Isabel Hageman
14 Oct 1772	Ferry, Thomas and Olly Davis

25 Jan 1810	Finney, Charles and Mary Corson
6 Jan 1808	Finney, Jesse and Elizabeth Craven
12 Feb 1761	Fisher, Doortye and Jacob Brant
24 Dec 1794	Folwell, Joseph and Lytie Lefferts
27 Mary 1765	Foster, Abraham and Agnes Barnes
28 Apr 1757	Fry, Catrina and John Godfrey Schach
9 Jan 1758	Gerrise, Annetye and Christophel Motsler
18 Aug 1772	Gissip, Elizabeth and John Kees
27 Jan 1763	Grant, John and Mary Campbell
24 Mar 1743/4	Grauser, Peter and Mary Vandegrift
31 Oct 1745	Green, Hannah and John Wiggman
21 Apr 1762	Gregg, James and Hannah Plumley
23 Mar 1744/5	Greuser, Peter and Maria Vandegrift
25 Jan 1801	Grier, Alexander and Hannah Merrick
10 Jun 1765	Hadley, Sarah and Joseph White
13 May 1742	Hafte, Benjamin and Ida Herman
19 May 1801	Hageman, Benjamin and Elizabeth Murray
23 Jun 1808	Hageman, Hannah and William Scott
11 Mar 1801	Hageman, Isabel and John M. Ferron
20 Oct 1741	Hageman, Jan and Jannetye VanHoorn
25 Jan 1769	Hageman, Jan and Martha VanHorn
13 Sep 1768	Hageman, Maria and David Feaster
28 Apr 1810	Hageman, Phoebe and Joseph Scott
30 Apr 1809	Hageman, Priscilla and Jacob Scott
25 Oct 1809	Hageman, Susanna and Jacob Warner
-- --- 1749	Halsworth, Elizabeth and Jacob Strickler
6 Mar 1771	Harding, Joseph and Martha Addis
24 Mar 1776	Harding, Martha and Walter Willet
23 Aug 1770	Hardy, Rachel and Mathias Fenton
10 Mar 1768	Harvey, Leah and Thomas Bulger
9 Jun 1763	Harvey, Sarah and Thomas Britton
22 Nov 1764	Hatton, John and Elizabeth Brees
10 Nov 1766	Headley, Samuel and Maria Betts
31 Mar 1744	Heaton, Anna and Roelf Dun
15 Apr 1747	Heaton, Robert and Ann Carvour
17 Feb 1761	Heeflinger, Andrew and Nettye Macbryan
16 May 1765	Hellings, John and Elizabeth Titus
30 Dec 1788	Henderson, Jane and Isaac Van Pelt
7 Dec 1767	Henry, Joseph and Esther Bigelow
13 May 1742	Herman, Ida and Benjamin Hafte
6 Apr 1743	Herman, Jane and Josiah Mattuck
26 Jan 1737/8	Hessing, Jacoba and Jan Karl

11 Apr 1761	Hibbs, Hannah and David Smith
22 Dec 1763	Hibbs, Isaac and Elizabeth Roberts
4 Dec 1760	Hibbs, Phoebe and Joseph Smith
5 Aug 1761	Hibbs, Zimmiah and Richard Parsons
13 Jan 1755	Hickman, Eva Catrina and John Wilhelm Cephard
10 Jan 1805	Hilburn, Joseph and Sarah Murray
12 Nov 1767	Hillebrant, Christophel and Maria Vansickelen
28 Nov 1749	Hillebrandt, Elizabeth and Hendrick Lymbacher
6 Feb 1766	Hillins, Mary and William Mannington
23 Dec 1804	Hitts, Hannah and Matthew Worrell
20 Jan 1757	Hoagland, Marytye and Jilus Kroesen
19 May 1753	Hofte, Catrytie and Jacob Vandergrift
30 Oct 1766	Hogeland, Catharine and Harman Vansant
12 Jan 1769	Hogeland, Derrick and Idah Bennet
5 Jun 1803	Hogeland, Derrick and Mary Van Pelt
7 Oct 1799	Hogeland, Jane and Benjamin Loder
14 Apr 1796	Hogeland, John and Margaret Powers
8 Jun 1804	Hogeland, John and Susanna Meyers
27 Sep 1789	Hogeland, Mary and Abraham Stevens
15 Sep 1805	Hogeland, Sarah and John Kroesen
3 Jun 1761	Hogeland, Daniel and Elsye Kroesen
18 Mar 1764	Hommer, Esther and William Worthington
10 Oct 1746	Hoof, Johannis and Antye Kroesen
19 Jun 1746	Houton, John and Esther Vandegrift
26 Apr 1769	Howard, Theodosia and Hugh Morton
17 Aug 1768	Huddleston, Henry and Elizabeth Bennet
8 May 1768	Huddleston, Joseph and Margaret Thomas
11 Oct 1762	Huddleston, Sarah and James Price
26 Aug 1763	Huddleston, Thomas and Elizabeth Slygar
10 Aug 1742	Hufte, Marcetye and Folkert Van De Grift
27 Aug 1810	Hunt, John and Sarah Scott
19 Nov 1789	Hunt, Joseph and Laetitia Kroesen
23 Apr 1771	Hunter, Andrew and Elizabeth Longshore
20 Mar 1799	Ishburn, Joseph and Atty Kroesen
1 Oct 1806	Jobes, William and Anne Romain
11 Jul 1799	Johnson, Elizabeth and John Fenton
21 Jun 1804	Johnson, Hannah and William Logan
27 Oct 1767	Johnson, John and Jane Erwin
19 Mar 1746/7	Johnson, Wilmot and Jacob Vandegrift
19 Feb 1801	Jolly, James and Jane McMasters
23 Dec 1761	Jones, Annitye and Jan Bennet
27 Sep 1799	Jones, Benjamin and Elizabeth Vanzant

27 May 1762	Jones, Henry and Nancy Anderson
5 Apr 1810	Jones, Jane and Cadwalader Erwin
27 Dec 1730	Juhambach, Jurich and Elizabeth Bohm
26 Jun 1737/8	Karl, Jan and Jacoba Hessing
5 Apr 1742	Keeler, Maria Eva and Hendrick Stoolryh
13 Aug 1772	Kees, John and Elizabeth Gissip
13 Mar 1766	Keith, Martha and James McNear
5 Apr 1772	Keyser, Christian and Jannetye Vanlinden
20 Mar 1799	Keyser, Kasper and Anna Corson
2 May 1765	Kinsey, George and Phaba Smith
25 Feb 1808	Kinsey, Mary and James Vansant
26 Jun 1766	Kirkbridge, Hannah and Willam Biles
26 Dec 1739	Klenklin, Marcillis and Hendrick Both
10 Apr 1771	Knoles, Joseph and Geertye Van Horn
6 Aug 1772	Knowles, Anna and Samuel Laurance
23 Aug 1757	Knowles, Lena and Aart. Bennet
23 Oct 1756	Koppen, Catrina and Rynaert Potts
5 Nov 1760	Kroesen, Adriene and Simon Cornell
25 Mar 1758	Kroesen, Adryante and Wilhelmus Nevins
10 Oct 1746	Kroesen, Antye and Johannis Hoof
20 Mar 1799	Kroesen, Atty and Joseph Ishburn
19 Aug 1804	Kroesen, Catherine and Joseph Fenton
31 Dec 1807	Kroesen, Catherine and Peter Lefferts
16 Jun 1753	Kroesen, Derrick and Elizabeth Vandegrift
31 Mar 1738/9	Kroesen, Dirck and Maria Vleit
20 Jan 1738/9	Kroesen, Elizabeth and Johannis Sleght
30 Apr 1742	Kroesen, Elizabeth and Jan Van Arsdalen
26 Oct 1748	Kroesen, Elizabeth and Stoffle Van Arsdalen
26 Jan 1796	Kroesen, Elizabeth and John Vanzant
17 Mar 1796	Kroesen, Elizabeth and Abraham Roberts
16 Nov 1809	Kroesen, Elizabeth and Gillian Cornell
3 Jun 1761	Kroesen, Elsye and Daniel Hogland
24 Dec 1789	Kroesen, Elsye and John Telford
14 Apr 1744	Kroesen, Essie and Wilhelm Cornel
6 Jun 1747	Kroesen, Franz and Jannetye Romain
21 Mar 1765	Kroesen, Garret and Leentye Fenton
19 Aug 1804	Kroesen, Isaac and Lydia Egbert
19 May 1753	Kroesen, Jacobus and Antye Nevins
17 Apr 1806	Kroesen, Jane and John Vanartsdalen
20 Jan 1757	Kroesen, Jilus and Marytye Hoagland
15 Sep 1805	Kroesen, John and Sarah Hogeland
19 Nov 1789	Kroesen, Laetitia and Joseph Hunt

24 Mar 1761	Kroesen, Lemmetye and Cornelius Wykoff
3 Nov 1801	Kroesen, Mary and William Bennet
15 Jul 1809	Kroesen, Mary and Æneas Tomlinson
29 Nov 1810	Kroesen, Mary and John Van Buskirk
16 Feb 1758	Krusen, Derrick and Maria Bennet
19 Dec 1766	Laning, Martha and Daniel Dougherty
28 Oct 1770	Larue, Isaac and Geertruy Stone
27 Apr 1769	Larue, Mary and Richard Stillwin
6 Mar 1804	Larzalere, Abraham and Martha Vankirk
7 Dec 1758	Lawrence, Lewis and Maria Severns
6 Aug 1772	Lawrence, Samuel and Anna Knowles
18 May 1768	Lee, David and Rebecca Sackel
7 Mar 1765	Leedom, Benjamin and Elise Pierson
28 Oct 1762	Leedom, Samuel and Hannah Staats
25 Nov 1810	Lefferts, Anne and Wilhelmus Cornell
28 Dec 1804	Lefferts, John and Helena Dubois
13 Oct 1808	Lefferts, John and Susanna Wynkoop
19 Nov 1789	Lefferts, Leffert and Nelly Dongan
24 Dec 1794	Lefferts, Lytie and Joseph Folwell
31 Dec 1807	Lefferts, Peter and Catharine Kroesen
6 Apr 1810	Lefferts, Simon and Mary Fenton
11 Jan 1770	Leffertse, Peter and Lammetye Vanartsdalen
18 Feb 1767	Leffertsen, Ares and Adrientye Vanartsdalen
5 Nov 1767	Lewis, Abraham and Elizabeth Doughty
25 Jun 1768	Lewis, Henry and Sarah Davis
30 Jan 1765	Linten, Samuel and Elizabeth Brees
7 Oct 1799	Loder, Benjamin and Janen Hogeland
1 Feb 1769	Logan, Dorcas and Alexander Miller
21 Jun 1804	Logan, William and Hannah Johnson
24 Nov 1789	Lombeart, Herman Joseph and Margaret Wynkoop
23 Apr 1771	Longshore, Elizabeth and Andrew Hunter
10 Dec 1767	Longshore, Elsie and John Paist
15 Apr 1801	Longstroth, Mary and Wm Wynkoop
29 Sep 1765	Loofborough, David and Sarah Twining
17 Feb 1763	Love, James and Hannah Russell
23 Nov 1763	Lubicee, Catrina and Samuel Price
28 Nov 1749	Lymbacher, Hendrick and Elizabeth Hillebrandt
13 Jan 1789	McCrum, William and Mary Feaster
31 Aug 1798	McGrady, Mary and John Marshall
18 Jul 1753	McInsley, Elizabeth and William Anderson
19 Feb 1801	McMasters, Jane and James Jolly
26 Nov 1800	McNair, Martha and Cornelius Van Horn

30 Dec 1799	McNeal, Elizabeth and John Ester
26 Dec 1764	McNear, Ann and John Vance
13 Mar 1766	McNear, James and Martha Keith
12 Jun 1801	McNear, Samuel and Cornelius Vanartsdalen
27 Oct 1768	McNies, Eleanor and Thomas Butterworth
24 Dec 1799	McRannels, James and Abbe Night
17 Feb 1761	Macbryan, Nettye and Andrew Heeflinger
17 May 1745	MacNough, John and Cathrina Van Pelt
6 Feb 1766	Mannington, William and Mary Hillins
31 Aug 1798	Marshall, John and Mary McGrady
11 Feb 1790	Matchner, John and Elizabeth Strickler
6 Apr 1743	Mattuck, Josiah and Jane Herman
30 Nov 1742	Mattuck, Martha and John Duffield
14 May 1766	Meir, Jacob and Elsye Van Pelt
25 Jan 1801	Merrick, Hannah and Alexander Grier
8 Jun 1804	Meyers, Susanna and John Hogeland
1 Feb 1769	Miller, Alexander and Dorcas Logan
8 Jun 1769	Mitchell, Samuel and Charity Brees
26 Apr 1769	Morton, Hugh and Theodosia Howard
10 Jan 1771	Morton, Hugh and Ann Crozier
9 Jan 1758	Motsler, Christophel and Annetye Gerrise
16 Dec 1765	Murdock, Joseph and Sarah Anderson
19 May 1801	Murray, Elizabeth and Benjamin Hageman
4 Nov 1801	Murray, Mary and Wilhelmus Corsen
6 Nov 1802	Murray, Samuel and Martha Briggs
10 Jan 1805	Murray, Sarah and Joseph Hilburn
3 Mar 1796	Nales, Isaac and Jane Vandeventer
20 Jan 1738/9	Navins, Cornelius and Sarah Sleght
15 Apr 1747	Naylor, Rachel and John Carvour
24 Jun 1766	Neeley, William and Elizabeth Thompson
31 Mar 1744	Neffers, Margriethe and Ryk Van Enden
19 May 1753	Nevins, Antye and Jacobus Kroesen
17 Feb 1763	Nevins, Catrina and Johannis Van Horn
7 Feb 1765	Nevins, Jores and Susanna Bogaet
25 Mar 1758	Nevins, Wilhelmus and Adriantye Kroesen
24 Dec 1799	Night, Abbe and James McRannels
6 Apr 1803	Night, Mary and Silas Vanzant
15 Apr 1747	Nixon, Lea and Garret Vansandt
10 Apr 1765	Nixon, Sarah and James Tompkins
4 Jan 1798	Nobles, Elizabeth and Jesse Edwards
23 Feb 1772	O'Neal, Deborah and Mathew Wisnor
4 Oct 1769	Osmond, Isaac and Rachel Powel

10 Dec 1767	Paist, John and Elsie Longshore
24 Jun 1804	Palmer, William and Mary Barrack
20 Mar 1768	Parson, George and Margaret Walmsley
5 Aug 1761	Parsons, Richard and Zimmiah Hibbs
23 May 1800	Paterson, Mary and John Dean
24 Jan 1768	Paxton, Phineas and Susanna Shaw
17 Mar 1762	Pearson, Margaret and Johannis Van Horn
7 Mar 1763	Pennington, Paul and Sarah Dooley
4 Oct 1770	Pettit, William and Sarah Burdsall
11 Jul 1771	Phillips, John and Esther Tod
7 Mar 1765	Pierson, Elise and Benjamin Leedom
21 Apr 1762	Plumley, Hannah and James Gregg
13 Aug 176	Plummer, Elizabeth and Christian Van Horn
17 Mar 1762	Plummer, William and Jane Yardley
14 Nov 1742	Pokinson, Maria and Baltus Ernst
23 Oct 1756	Potts, Rynaert and Catrina Koppen
4 Oct 1769	Powel, Rachel and Isaac Osmond
14 Apr 1796	Powers, Margaret and John Hogeland
20 Jan 1757	Praal, Johannis and Geertye Vandegrift
18 Dec 1766	Prawl, Jenneke and Arent Schuyler
11 Oct 1762	Price, James and Sarah Huddleston
31 Sep 1770	Price, Margaret and Benjamin Sargeant
23 Nov 1763	Price, Samuel and Catrina Lubicee
2 May 1802	Puff, Elizabeth and Isaac Rutherford
23 Apr 1771	Quimby, Phoebe and Ambrose Barcroft
17 Aug 1790	Raguet, James and Anna Wynkoop
2 Jul 1807	Raine, Rachel and Brittain Evans
25 Oct 1759	Randall, George and Mary Dunn
16 Sep 1810	Randall, John and Elizabeth Vansant
3 Nov 1801	Randolph, Joseph and Mary Bennet
8 Mar 1801	Randolph, Phoebe and John Vanartsdalen
22 May 1796	Reeder, Abner and Hannah Wilkinson
23 Feb 1772	Reeder, Benjamin and Presylah Rose
27 Sep 1772	Remise, Phillippus and Rachel Van -----
6 May 1753	Renise, Aaltyle and Wykoff Van Nordsbrant
20 Sep 1810	Renton, Margaret and William Vancout
15 Oct 1761	Rice, Catrina and Conrad Schiver
11 Jan 1803	Rich, Hannah and George Tomilson
17 May 1769	Richardson, Samuel and Jesinah Rue
23 Nov 1761	Rickey, Mary and John Derbyshire
23 Apr 1771	Rise, Edward and Hannah Barcroft
10 Jan 1805	Roats, Anna and John White

19 Oct 1806	Roats, John and Cornelia Van Pelt
28 May 1765	Roberson, William and Sarah Beebe
17 Mar 1796	Roberts, Abraham and Elizabeth Kroesen
4 Dec 1760	Roberts, Elizabeth and Tunia Titus
22 Dec 1763	Roberts, Elizabeth and Isaac Hibbs
13 Feb 1766	Roberts, Johannis and Jannetye Bennet
8 Oct 1800	Roberts, Phoebe and James Thompson
31 Mar 1763	Roberts Samuel and Mary Eastburn
31 Oct 1805	Rodman, John and Mary Street
1 Oct 1806	Romain, Anne and William Jobes
6 Jun 1747	Romain, Jannetye and Franz Kroesen
25 Nov 1738	Roos, Hendrick and Susanna Adams
23 Feb 1772	Rose, Presylah and Benjamin Reeder
5 Jan 1769	Rue, Elizabeth and Daniel Severns
17 May 1769	Rue, Jesinah and Samuel Richardson
15 Mar 1769	Rue, Lewis and Ruth Whight
27 Mar 1745/6	Rue, Samuel and Aaltye Van Sand
17 Feb 1763	Russel, Hannah and James Love
2 May 1802	Rutherford, Isaac and Elizabeth Puff
6 Nov 1800	Ruthford, Mary and Wm Stogden
18 May 1768	Sackel, Rebecca and David Lee
21 Dec 1763	Sackett, Klartye and Simon Bennet
31 Sep 1770	Sargeant, Benjamin and Margaret Price
28 Apr 1757	Schach, John Godfrey and Catrina Fry
22 Feb 1759	Schefer, Johannis and Catryntye Sleght
15 Oct 1761	Schiver, Conrad and Catrina Rice
18 Dec 1766	Schuyler, Arent and Jenneke Prawl
30 Apr 1809	Scott, Jacob and Priscilla Hageman
28 Apr 1810	Scott, Joseph and Phoebe Hageman
27 Aug 1810	Scott, Sarah and John Hunt
23 Jun 1808	Scott, William and Hannah Hageman
18 Apr 1758	Sedam, Jannetye and Ryk Bennet
2 Jan 1741/2	Sedam, Maria and Benjamin Corson
17 Mar 1808	Sevens, Jabez and Jemima Bretsford
5 Jan 1769	Severns, Daniel and Elizabeth Rue
7 Dec 1758	Severns, Maria and Lawrence Lewis
7 Apr 1762	Shamp, Johannis M. and Catryna Sleght
24 Jan 1768	Shaw, Susannah and Phineas Paxton
18 Apr 1770	Shee, Sarah and Joseph Wright
3 Apr 1806	Shelmire, David and Jane Vansant
20 Apr 1769	Sibbett, Robert and Margaret Barnet
23 May 1745	Simonsen, Fermertye and Johannes Vandegrift

12 Nov 1801	Simonson, John and Margaret Swain
30 Dec 1760	Sirl, Rebecca and William Carter
18 Mar 1768	Skinner, Reuben and Elizabeth Woods
13 Nov 1740	Slecht, Cornelia and Johannis Van Pelt
16 Jun 1768	Sleght, Abraham and Martha Titus
7 Apr 1762	Sleght, Catryna and Johannis M. Shamp
22 Feb 1759	Slight, Catryntye and Johannis Schefer
1 Nov 1764	Sleght, Janneke and Barent Van Horn
20 Jan 1738/9	Sleght, Johannis and Elizabeth Kroeser
20 Jan 1738/9	Sleght, Sarah and Cornelius Navins
26 Aug 1763	Slygar, Elizabeth and Thomas Huddleston
11 Apr 1761	Smith, David and Hannah Hibbs
7 Apr 1800	Smith, John and Martha Fenton
4 Dec 1760	Smith, Joseph and Phoebe Hibbs
2 May 1765	Smith, Phaba and George Kinsey
20 Nov 1788	Smock, Sarah and Jacob Vanartsdalen
1 Jul 1741	Snowden, Elizabeth and Johannis Van De Grist
4 Apr 1763	Stocher, Massey and John Baldwin
27 Nov 1764	Squire, Michael and Catrina Waits
28 Oct 1762	Staats, Hannah and Samuel Leedom
29 Jan 1766	Stackhouse, Esther and Daniel Wright
5 Dec 1744	Staghers, Jacob and ----- -----
27 Sep 1789	Stevens, Abraham and Mary Hogeland
18 Jul 1800	Stevens, Benjamin and Sarah Van Horn
19 Apr 1770	Stevens, Catharine and John Blake
9 Jun 1763	Stevens, Johannis and Sarah Stoothoff
4 May 1758	Stevens, Maria and Carrol Engard
27 Apr 1769	Stillwin, Richard and Mary Larue
24 Mar 1763	Stogdale, Robert and Mary Willard
6 Nov 1800	Stogden, William and Mary Ruthford
28 Oct 1770	Stone, Geertruy and Isaac Larue
5 Apr 1742	Stoolryh, Hendrich and Maria Eva Keeler
9 Jun 1763	Stoothoff, Sarah and Johannis Stevens
23 Oct 1766	Stout, Rachel and William Clawson
31 Oct 1805	Street, Mary and John Rodman
8 Mar 1804	Street, Nathan and Sarah Vanzant
21 Sep 1749	Strickler, Elizabeth and Mathew Arsen
11 Feb 1790	Strickler, Elizabeth and John Matchner
-- --- 1749	Strickler, Jacob and Elizabeth Halsworth
12 Jan 1764	Subers, Johannis and Catrina Van Horn
12 Nov 1801	Swain, Margaret and John Simonson
18 Oct 1742	Swarks, Maria and Johannis Butcher

16 Aug 1785	Sweetser, Benjamin and Esther Bross
25 May 1795	Taggert, David and Helen Du Boise
20 Jul 1763	Terry, David and Grace Davis
11 Dec 1739	Thielsheren, Hans Michael and Marsilis Cassidan
8 May 1768	Thomas, Margaret and Joseph Huddleston
5 Dec 1745	Thomas, Maria and William Bartholomew
20 Feb 1745/6	Thomas, Martha and Jonathan Drake
24 Jun 1766	Thompson, Elizabeth and William Neely
8 Oct 1800	Thompson, James and Phoebe Roberts
15 Jan 1761	Thornton, Joseph and Elizabeth Willet
16 May 1765	Titus, Elizabeth and John Hellings
16 Jun 1768	Titus, Martha and Abraham Sleght
1 Nov 1770	Titus, Samuel and Deborah Feathers
4 Dec 1760	Titus, Tunis and Elizabeth Roberts
11 Jul 1771	Tod, Esther and John Philips
11 Jan 1803	Tomilson, George and Hannah Rich
10 Apr 1765	Tomkins, James and Sarah Nixon
15 Jul 1809	Tomlinson, Æneas and Mary Kroesen
26 Nov 1810	Tomlinson, Joseph and Elizabeth Walton
26 May 1801	Turner, William and Jane Burlay
29 Sep 1765	Twining, Sarah and David Loofborough
27 Sep 1772	Van -----, Rachel and Phillippus Remise
30 Apr 1742	Van Arsdalen, Jan and Elizabeth Kroesen
20 Dec 1759	Vanarsdalen, Nicholas and Jannetye Vansant
18 Feb 1767	Vanartsdalen, Adrietye and Ares Leffertsen
4 Nov 1789	Van Artsdalen, Christopher and Phoebe Vanzant
12 Jun 1801	Vanartsdalen, Cornelia and Samuel McNear
25 Jun 1809	Vanartsdalen, Hannah and Richard Corson
14 Jun 1810	Vanartsdalen, Henry and Jane Corson
10 Nov 1788	Vanartsdalen, Jacob and Sarah Smock
25 May 1795	Vanartsdalen, John and Mary Fenton
8 Mar 1801	Vanartsdalen, John and Phoebe Randolph
17 Apr 1806	Vanartsdalen, John and Jane Kroesen
11 Jan 1770	Vanartsdalen, Lammetye and Peter Leffertse
20 Dec 1800	Van Artsdalen, Margaret and Jesse Williard
25 May 1795	Vanartsdalen, Mary and Joseph Fenton
26 Oct 1748	Van Arsdalen, Stoffle and Elizabeth Kroesen
28 Apr 1744	Van Boskirk, Garret and Maria Van Lazen
29 Nov 1810	Van Buskirk, John and Mary Kroesen
26 Dec 1764	Vance, John and Ann McNear
20 Sep 1810	Vancourt, William and Margaret Renton
3 Jul 1760	Vandergrift, Cornelius and Elizabeth Vansant

16 Jun 1753	Vandegrift, Elizabeth and Derrick Kroesen
19 Jun 1746	Vandergrift, Esther and John Houton
10 Aug 1742	Van DeGrift, Folkert and Marcetye Hufte
20 Jan 1757	Vandegrift, Geertye and Johannis Praal
19 Mar 1746/7	Vandegrift, Jacob and Wilmot Johnson
19 May 1753	Vandegrift, Jacob and Catrytie Hofte
1 Jul 1741	Van DeGrift, Johannis and Elizabeth Snowden
23 May 1745	Vandegrift, Johannis and Fermertye Simonsen
5 Dec 1809	Vandegrift, Margaret and James Cornell
24 Mar 1743/4	Vandegrift, Mary and Peter Grauser
23 Mar 1744/5	Vandegrift, Maria and Peter Grauser
26 Jun 1746	Vandegrift, Rebecca and Ralter Van Schyyen
3 Mar 1796	Vandeventer, Jane and Isaac Nales
14 Sep 1754	Van Dyke, Margaritta and Isaac Bennet
14 Oct 1762	Vandyke, Maria and Jacob Wimmer
16 Feb 1755	Van Enden, Margaritta and Cornelius Corson
31 Mar 1744	Van Enden, Ryk and Margriethe Neffers
31 Dec 1741	Van Hoorn, Barent and Jannetye Booskirk
29 Jul 1742	Van Hoorn, Guertrie and Andries Boskirk
20 Oct 1741	Van Hoorn, Jannetye and Jan Hageman
12 May 1739	Van Hoorn, Johannis and Lena Van Pelt
24 Mar 1772	Van Horn, Abraham and Leentye Bennet
17 Jan 1752/3	Van Horn, Barent and Sarah Van Pelt
1 Nov 1764	Van Horn, Barent and Janneke Sleght
12 Jan 1764	Van Horn, Catrina and Johannis Subers
13 Aug 1761	Van Horn, Christian and Elizabeth Plummer
14 Jun 1764	Van Horn, Christian and Sarah Vansant
26 Nov 1800	Van Horn, Cornelius and Martha McNair
10 Apr 1771	Van Horn, Geertye and Joseph Knowles
3 Apr 1755	Van Horn, Jane and Jeremiah Van Horn
3 Apr 1755	Van Horn, Jeremiah and Jane Van Horn
17 Mar 1762	Van Horn, Johannis and Margaret Pearson
17 Feb 1763	Van Horn, Johannis and Catrina Nevins
7 Apr 1802	Van Horn, Margareta and Joseph Willet
17 Oct 1745	Van Horn, Maria and Isaac Bennet
25 Jan 1769	Van Horn, Martha and Jan Hageman
18 Jul 1800	Van Horn, Sarah and Benjamin Stevens
6 Mar 1804	Van Kirk, Martha and Abraham Larzalere
28 Apr 1744	Van Lazen, Maria and Garret Van Boskirk
5 Apr 1772	Vanlinden, Jannetye and Christian Keyser
6 May 1753	Van Nordsbrant, Wykoff and Aaltyle Renise
17 May 1745	Van Pelt, Cathrina and John MacNough

19 Oct 1806	Van Pelt, Cornelia and John Roats
8 Apr 1732	Van Pelt, Elizabeth and Johannis Bennet
14 May 1776	Van Pelt, Elsye and Jacob Meyer
30 Dec 1788	Van Pelt, Isaac and Jane Henderson
13 Nov 1740	Van Pelt, Johannis and Cornelia Slecht
12 May 1739	Van Pelt, Lena and Johannis Van Hoorn
5 Jun 1803	Van Pelt, Mary and Derrick Hogeland
17 Jan 1752/3	Van Pelt, Sarah and Barent Van Horn
27 Mar 1745/6	Van Sand, Aaltye and Samuel Rue
15 Apr 1747	Vansandt, Garret and Lea Nixon
3 Jul 1760	Vansant, Elizabeth and Cornelius Vandergrift
16 Sep 1810	Vansant, Elizabeth and John Randall
30 Oct 1766	Vansant, Harman and Catharine Hogeland
23 Aug 1756	Vansant, Jacobus and Jannetye Bennet
25 Feb 1808	Vansant, James and Mary Kinsey
3 Apr 1806	Vansant, Jane and David Shelmire
20 Dec 1659	Vansant, Jennetye and Nicholas Vanarsdalen
14 Jun 1764	Van Sant, Sarah and Christian Van Horn
26 Jun 1746	Van Schyven, Ralter and Rebecca Vandergrift
11 Jun 1756	Van Sicklen, Jannetye and Benjamin Bennet
12 Nov 1767	Vansickelen, Maria and Christopel Hillebrant
12 Apr 1801	Vanzant, Atty and James Vanzant
11 Sep 1789	Vanzant, Eleanor and John Brown
27 Sep 1799	Vanzant, Elizabeth and Benjamin Jones
12 Apr 1801	Vanzant, James and Atty Vanzant
9 Oct 1806	Vanzant, Jane and David Walton
26 Jan 1796	Vanzant, John and Elizabeth Kroesen
4 Nov 1789	Vanzant, Phoebe and Christopher Van Artsdalen
8 Mar 1804	Vanzant, Sarah and Nathan Street
6 Apr 1803	Vanzant, Silas and Mary Night
5 Mar 1789	Vanzant, William and Jane Bennet
31 Mar 1788/9	Vleit, Maria and Dirck Kroesen
27 Nov 1764	Waits, Catrina and Michael Squire
20 Mar 1763	Walmsley, Margaret and George Parson
3 Jun 1807	Walton, Abraham and Euphemia Wilson
9 Oct 1806	Walton, David and Jane Vanzant
26 Nov 1810	Walton, Elizabeth and Joseph Tomlinson
25 Oct 1809	Warner, Jacob and Susanna Hageman
31 Dec 1746	Waters, William and Deborah Ashton
5 Nov 1769	Welsh, James and Jane Chandler
25 Apr 1769	West, Charity and Adam Barr
15 Mar 1769	Whight, Ruth and Lewis Rue

16 Apr 1765 White, Elizabeth and Hendrick Bennett
10 Jan 1805 White, John and Anna Roats
10 Jun 1765 White, Joseph and Sarah Hadley
31 Oct 1745 Wiggman, John and Hannah Green
22 May 1796 Wilkinson, Hannah and Abner Reeder
13 Oct 1766 Willet, Catharine and Joshua Comley
15 Jan 1760 Willet, Elizabeth and Joseph Thornton
7 Apr 1802 Willet, Joseph and Margaretta Van Horn
24 Mar 1766 Willet, Walter and Martha Harding
20 Dec 1800 Williard, Jesse and Margaret Vanartsdalen
24 Mar 1763 Willard, Mary and Robert Stogdale
13 Dec 1767 Williamson, Hannah and Samuel Yardley
11 Aug 1763 Williamson, Jesse and Sarah Britton
3 Jun 1807 Wilson, Euphemia and Abraham Walton
14 Oct 1762 Wimmer, Jacob and Maria Vandyk
23 Feb 1772 Wisnor, Matthew and Deborah O'Neal
18 Mar 1768 Woods, Elizabeth and Reuben Skinner
23 Dec 1804 Worrell, Matthew and Hannah Hilts
1 Nov 1804 Worthington, John and Elizabeth Comely
25 Jan 1767 Worthington, Joseph and Elizabeth Carver
18 Mar 1764 Worthington, William and Esther Hommer
29 Jan 1766 Wright, Daniel and Esther Stackhouse
18 Apr 1770 Wright, Joseph and Sarah Shee
24 Mar 1766 Wykoff, Cornelius and Lammety Kroesen
12 May 1757 Wykoff, Gerardus and Elizabeth Bennet
15 Feb 1790 Wylley, David and Susanna Wynkoop
17 Aug 1790 Wynkoop, Anna and James Raguet
7 Dec 1758 Wynkoop, Garret and Elizabeth Bennet
18 Dec 1751 Wynkoop, Helletye and Jonathan Du Bois
24 Nov 1789 Wynkoop, Margaretta and Joseph Herman Lombeart
15 Feb 1790 Wynkoop, Susanna and David Wylley
13 Oct 1808 Wynkoop, Susanna and John Lefferts
15 Apr 1801 Wynkoop, William and Mary Longstroth
17 Mar 1762 Yardley, Jane and William Plummer
13 Dec 1767 Yardley, Samuel and Hannah Williamson

Hilltown Baptist Church, Upper Church and Stump Road. Hilltown Twp. Minutes 1781-1800.

Persons to be dismissed on 10 Nov 1782 from us for the purpose of being constituted a regular Gospel Church in Hilltown ...

Rev. John Thomas; Sarah Thomas; Manasseth Thomas; Enoch Thomas; Sarah Thomas; Job Thomas; Rebecca Thomas; Amos Thomas; Ruth Thomas; Thomas Mathias; Elizabeth Mathias; John Mathias; Alice Mathias; Jeremiah Vastine; Elizabeth Vastine; Joseph Brittain; Abigail Brittain; Nathl. Brittain; Rachel Brittain; Elijah Davis; Elizabeth Davies; John Brittain, Senr.; Joseph Eaton; James Morgan; Thomas Jones; Elijah Brittain; Moses Aaron; Nathan Evans; Isaac Freeman; Evan Pugh; Rebecca Pugh; Rachel Harding; Sarah Thomas; Eleanor Thomas; Sarah Thomas; Mary Thomas; Margaret Jones; Ann Young; Hannah Kastner; Mary Riale; Mary Griffith; Margaret Jones; Gwently Morris; Alice Lunn; Anna Brittain; Hannah Mathias; Sarah Parker; Mary Eaton; Rachel Morris; Mary Nelson; Mary Lewis; Ann Smith; Catharine Philips - and that when they shall be so constituted, they will be fully dismissed from us, and how we Pray they may be abundantly blessed of the Lord, made a fruitful nursery, and a mother in Isreal. Signed, Thomas Davis, Isaac James eld., Joseph Griffith, Peter Evans, Christopher Wells, Henry Haer?.

15 Oct 1785. Abner Davies bapt.

17 Aug 1786. Joseph Morris and Dorothy James bapt.

16 Sep 1786. Thomas Jones Junr., Jonathan Jones and John James bapt.

15 Oct 1786. Humphrey Williams excluded from church fellowship.

16 Dec 1786. John Smith received by letter and Amos Thomas and Ruth his wife dismissed by letter.

Oct 1787. James Eaton received by letter. Brother Jeremiah Vastine removed by death.

Marcy 1788. John Smith suspended.

19 April 1788. John Smith admitted. He requested a letter of dismission - granted.

20 Dec 1788. Martha Philips (formerly Davies) having removed to the Great

Valley, requested a letter of dismission. granted. Robert Shannon and Isaac Hill appointed to receive several sums of money laid upon each member toward defraying the expense of the Iron bar?

18 April 1789. Joseph Morris restored to the fellowship of the church.

15 Aug 1789. Job Thomas to be admitted to former privileges with the church. Rev. James McLaughlin proposed to settle amongst us and to supply us three Lords days in a month for the term of one year.

19 Sep 1787. Anna Mathias, Nathan Mathias and Catharine Owen bapt.

Oct 1789. Mary Eaton, Mary Griffith and Rachel Brittain removed by death this year.

17 Oct 1789. Elijah Britain and his wife Jane and Hannah Eaton (alias Harris) dismissed.

16 Jan 1790. Sarah Parker made a gift of 3 dollars to the Church. Sarah Parker applied for a dismission to join a church in VA. Granted.

1 April 1790 Mary Morris bapt. and Sarah Mitchell examined.

18 May 1790. Enos Morris, Sarah Mitchel, Mary Godshalk and Anna Brittain Junr. bapt.

20 June 1790. Morgan Custer bapt. John James and his wife Dorothy dismissed.

18 Sep 1790. Charles Miller and his wife Catharine, Thomas Mathias, Thomas Thomas, Gainer Mathias and Elizabeth Morris bapt. Received members Joseph Brittain and Abigail his wife. Nathaniel Brittain and his wife Rachel were dismissed. Jonathan Jones and Rebecca Freeman removed by death this year.

Oct 1791. Received by baptisms this year Joshua Dungan, Asa Thomas, Adah Thomas and Elizabeth Godshalk. Nathan Mathias dismissed by letter. Rev. John Thomas removed by death who departed this life on 31 Oct 1790.

29 April 1790. John James and his wife Dorothy dismissed.

14 April 1792. Joseph Eaton and Rebecca Easton dismissed.

11 Dec 1792. Sister Freeman restored to the fellowship of the Church.

20 April 1793. Enoch Thomas and his wife obtained letters of recommendation. To enquire into the past conduct of Sarah Murphy.

On 18 May 1793. Sarah Murphy says she knew not of her husband's marriage with another till lately and agreed that she be under censure.

20 July 1793. Lydia Lester brought a letter of dismission from Philadelphia Baptist Church and was received. Sarah intends to continue with her husband agreeably to marriage. Abner Davies requested a letter of recommendation from this church. Granted.

14 Sep 1793. Informed that Mr. McLaughlin had been with the former wife of Isaac Murphy, who had shewn him a certificate of her marriage with Murphy.

14 Dec 1793. Sarah Murphy excluded.

20 Sep 1794. Elizabeth Harding to be bapt. tomorrow morning. Elizabeth Vastine and Joseph Thomas for past conduct laid under the censure of this church.

3rd Saturday Oct 1795. All is amicably settled between Joseph Thomas and Elizabeth Vastine.

17 Sep 1796. Lewis Bitting, William H. Rowland and Mary Rowland were examined and approved. Sarah Mathias, Anne Mathias and Sarah Ferrel were bapt. this year.

15 Oct 1796. Abel Mathias, Elizabeth Williams and Jane Davis were examined and approved. Present number 107.

19 Nov 1796. Joseph Thomas, Thomas Mathias, and Margaret Mathias were approved.

20 Aug 1797. Ann James was examined and received.

25 July 1797. Ann Mathias, wife of Thomas Mathias, mercht., dec'd.

17 Dec 1797. Moses Aaron requested a dismission. Granted.

15 June 1798. Joseph Lunn desired a dismission from this to the Church of Montgomery. Granted. Isaac Morris to enquire of the past misconduct of Joseph Thomas and his wife Mary. Elizabeth Davis and Martha Smith received by baptism.

18 Sep 1798. Joseph Thomas charges the Church with having dealt by him unjust and imprudent. Mary acknowledges her neglect and promises to return to her duty.

15 Dec 1798. Brother Evan Pugh died.
2 Jan 1799. Brother Isaac Hill died.
10 Jan 1799. Brother John Davies, Esq., died.

16 March 1799. Sister Sarah Darrah to be laid under the censure of the Church for her past conduct towards it.

29 April 1799. Brother Thomas Mathias Senr. died.

18 May 1799. Brother Joseph Morris suspended for his neglect toward the church.

11 Aug 1799. John Mathias (joiner) and his wife Eleanor bapt.

17 Aug 1799. John Mathias (yeoman), Sarah Heaton, Eleanor Thomas and Sarah Mathias bapt.

15 Sep 1799 Ashbel Jones and Margaret Bitting, wife of Lewis Bitting bapt.

30 Sep 1799. Isaac Williams, Benjamin Williams and his wife Eleanor, Thomas Williams, Joseph Mathias, Thomas Lunn and his wife Elizabeth bapt.

19 Oct 1799. Abraham Black and his wife Margaret, Elizabeth Griffith (wife of Howell Griffith) and Elizabeth Morris (wife of Mason Morris) bapt. Elizabeth Dungan (wife of William Dungan) applied for a letter of dismission to the Baptist church in Baltimore. Granted.

16 Nov 1799. Mary Thomas (wife of Doctr. Thomas), Ann Jones (wife of Wm. Jones), Margaret Miller (wife of P. Miller), Rachel Davis, Elias Black, Elizabeth Black, Wm.Thomas, Wm. Thomas Junr., Mary Morris Junr., Ann Sliver, examined. Bapt. next day.

7 Dec 1799. Lewis Lunn, Eleazer Bitting, Wm.Williams, Stephen Rowland

Junr., Rachel Morris and Martha Morris examined. Bapt. next day.

14 Dec 1799. David Thomas, John Young, Septimus Evans, Robert Shannon Junr., Mary Powel, Anna Fulton, Emma Lunn (wife of Elisha Lunn) and Huldah Morris were bapt. Sister Mary Lewis applied for a dismission - granted.

8 Feb 1800. Abigail Bitting, Hannah Shannon, Abigail Dodson, Catharine Owen, Rebekah Williams, and Jehu Miller were examined. Bapt. next day.

15 Feb 1800. May Bitting was examined and bapt. next day.

19 April 1800. Peter Medary, Catharine Owen, Ann Owen and Sarah Miller were examined, approved and bapt. Sister Rebekah James applied for a letter of dismission from this to Newbritain Church - granted. Sister Mary Powel applied for a letter of dismission from this to the Church in Phila. - granted.

14 June 1800. Suspension of Sarah Darrah removed. Tacy McLaughlin (wife of Pastor James McLaughlin) was received by letter from the Church of the Great Valley. Sister Sidney Thomas applied for dismission from this to the Church at Newbritain - granted.

16 Aug 1800. Joshua Dungan excluded.

8 Aug 1800. Sister Ann Smith died.
11 Sep 1800. Brother James Morgan died.

18 Oct 1800. Rebeccah Brown, Rebekah Mathias (wife of John Mathias) and Rachel Mathew (wife of John Mathew) examined and bapt. next day. Brother Enoch Thomas and his wife Sarah applied for a letter of recommendation - granted.

Rachel Harding b. 29 May 1744 (OS), d. 15 Jan 1842, aged 96-7-5. She survived all the other constituent members (who founded the Hilltown Church).

Most of the following was faint and difficult to read:
Rev. John Thomas d. 21 Oct 1790.
Job Thomas d. June 1798
Thomas Mathias d. 25 April 1790 (?)

Evan Pugh d. 15 Dec 1798
Elizabeth Davies d. 3 Oc 1785
Mary Thomas d. May 1793
Gwently Morris d. 3 Oct 1785
Mary Eaton d. 1789
Mary Lewis d. 1783
Abigail Black d. 1783
John Davies Senr. d. 10 Jan 1799
Isaac Hill d. 2 Jan 1799
Jonathan Jones d. May 1790

INDEX

Heritage Books by F. Edward Wright:

18th Century Records of the German Lutheran Church at Philadelphia, Pennsylvania (St. Michael's and Zion): Volume 1, Baptisms, 1745–1769
Robert L. Hess and F. Edward Wright

18th Century Records of the German Lutheran Church at Philadelphia, Pennsylvania (St. Michael's and Zion): Volume 2, Baptisms, 1770–1786
Translated by Robert L. Hess, Ph.D. Edited by F. Edward Wright

18th Century Records of the German Lutheran Church of Philadelphia, Pennsylvania (St. Michael's and Zion): Volume 3, Baptisms, 1787–1800
Translated by Robert L. Hess, Ph.D. Edited by F. Edward Wright

18th Century Records of the German Lutheran Church at Philadelphia, Pennsylvania (St. Michael's and Zion): Volume 4, Marriages and Confirmations
Robert L. Hess and F. Edward Wright

18th Century Records of the German Lutheran Church at Philadelphia, Pennsylvania (St. Michael's and Zion): Volume 5, Burials
Robert L. Hess and F. Edward Wright

Abstracts of Bucks County, Pennsylvania, Wills, 1685–1785

Abstracts of Cumberland County, Pennsylvania, Wills, 1750–1785

Abstracts of Cumberland County, Pennsylvania, Wills, 1785–1825

Abstracts of Philadelphia County, Pennsylvania, Wills:
Volumes: 1682–1726; 1726–1747; 1748–1763; 1763–1784; 1777–1790; 1790–1802; 1802–1809; 1810–1815; 1815–1819; and 1820–1825

Abstracts of South Central Pennsylvania, Newspapers, Volume 1, 1785–1790

Abstracts of South Central Pennsylvania, Newspapers, Volume 3, 1796–1800

Abstracts of the Newspapers of Georgetown and the Federal City, 1789–99

Abstracts of York County, Pennsylvania, Wills, 1749–1819

Adams County [Pennsylvania] Church Records of the 18th Century

Baltimore Directory of 1807

Berks County, Pennsylvania, Church Records of the 18th Century, Volumes 1–4

Bible Records of Washington County, Maryland

Bucks County, Pennsylvania, Church Records of the 17th and 18th Centuries, Volume 1: German Church Records

Bucks County, Pennsylvania, Church Records of the 17th and 18th Centuries, Volume 2: Quaker Records: Falls and Middletown Monthly Meetings
Anna Miller Watring and F. Edward Wright

Bucks County, Pennsylvania, Church Records of the 17th and 18th Centuries, Volume 4

Caroline County, Maryland, Marriages, Births and Deaths, 1850–1880

Citizens of the Eastern Shore of Maryland, 1659–1750

Colonial Families of Cape May County, New Jersey, Revised 2nd Edition

Colonial Families of Delaware:
Volumes: Volume 1; Volume 2: Kent and Sussex Counties;
Volume 3 (2nd Edition): Kent and Sussex Counties;
Volume 4: Sussex County; Volume 5: New Castle; Volume 6: Kent County

Colonial Families of New Jersey, Volume 1: Middlesex and Somerset Counties

Colonial Families of Northern Neck, Virginia, Volume 1 and Volume 2
Holly G. Wright and F. Edward Wright

Colonial Families of the Eastern Shore of Maryland: Volumes 1 and 2
Robert W. Barnes and F. Edward Wright

Colonial Families of the Eastern Shore of Maryland: Volume 4
Christos Christou and F. Edward Wright

Colonial Families of the Eastern Shore of Maryland:
Volumes 5, 6, 7, 8, 9, 11, 12, 13, 14, 16, and 19
Henry C. Peden, Jr. and F. Edward Wright

Colonial Families of the Eastern Shore of Maryland: Volumes 15 and 17
Ralph A. Riggin and F. Edward Wright

Colonial Families of the Eastern Shore of Maryland: Volumes 10, 18, 20, and 22
Vernon L. Skinner, Jr. and F. Edward Wright

Colonial Families of the United States of America, Volume II
Holly G. Wright and F. Edward Wright

Cumberland County, Pennsylvania, Church Records of the 18th Century

Delaware Newspaper Abstracts, Volume 1: 1786–1795

Early Charles County, Maryland, Settlers, 1658–1745
Marlene Strawser Bates, F. Edward Wright

Early Church Records of Alexandria City and Fairfax County, Virginia
F. Edward Wright and Wesley E. Pippenger

Early Church Records of Bergen County, New Jersey, 1740–1800

Early Church Records of Dauphin County, Pennsylvania

Early Church Records of Lebanon County, Pennsylvania

Early Church Records of New Castle County, Delaware, Volume 1: 1701–1800

Early Church Records of Rockingham County, Virginia

Early Church Records of Somerset County, New Jersey, Volume 1

Early Lists of Frederick County, Maryland, 1765–1775

Early Records of the First Reformed Church of Philadelphia, Volume 1, 1748–1780

Early Records of the First Reformed Church of Philadelphia, Volume 2, 1781–1800

Frederick County, Maryland, Militia in the War of 1812
Sallie A. Mallick and F. Edward Wright

Henrico County, Virginia, Marriage References and Family Relationships, 1654–1800

Inhabitants of Baltimore County, Maryland, 1692–1763

Judgment Records of Dorchester, Queen Anne's, and Talbot Counties [Maryland]

Kent County, Delaware, Marriage References and Family Relationships

King George County, Virginia, Marriage References
and Family Relationships, 1721–1800
Anne M. Watring and F. Edward Wright

Lancaster County Church Records of the 18th Century, Volumes 1–4

Lancaster County, Pennsylvania, Church Records of the 18th Century, Volume 1
F. Edward Wright and Robert L. Hess

Lancaster County, Pennsylvania, Church Records of the 18th Century, Volume 3

Lancaster County, Pennsylvania, Church Records of the 18th Century, Volume 5

Lancaster County, Pennsylvania, Church Records of the 18th Century: Volume 6
Robert L. Hess and F. Edward Wright

Lancaster County, Virginia, Marriage References and Family Relationships, 1650–1800

Land Records of Sussex County, Delaware, 1769–1782

Land Records of Sussex County, Delaware, 1782–1789: Deed Book N No. 13
Elaine Hastings Mason and F. Edward Wright

Marriage Licenses of Washington, District of Columbia, 1811–1830

Marriage References and Family Relationships of Charles City,
Prince George, and Dinwiddie Counties, Virginia, 1634–1800

Marriages and Deaths from Eastern Shore Newspapers, 1790–1835

Marriages and Deaths from the Newspapers of Allegany
and Washington Counties, Maryland, 1820–1830

Marriages and Deaths from the York Recorder, *1821–1830*

Marriages and Deaths in the Newspapers of Frederick
and Montgomery Counties, Maryland, 1820–1830

Marriages and Deaths in the Newspapers of
Lancaster County, Pennsylvania, 1821–1830

Marriages and Deaths in the Newspapers of
Lancaster County, Pennsylvania, 1831–1840

Marriages and Deaths of Cumberland County, [Pennsylvania], 1821–1830

Marriages, Births, Deaths and Removals of New Castle County, Delaware, 1801–1850

Maryland Calendar of Wills:
Volume 9: 1744–1749; Volume 10: 1748–1753; Volume 11: 1753–1760;
Volume 12: 1759–1764; Volume 13: 1764–1767; Volume 14: 1767–1772;
Volume 15: 1772–1774; and Volume 16: 1774–1777

Maryland Eastern Shore Newspaper Abstracts
Volume 1: 1790–1805; Volume 2: 1806–1812;
Volume 3: 1813–1818; Volume 4: 1819–1824;
Volume 5: Northern Counties, 1825–1829
F. Edward Wright and Irma Harper;
Volume 6: Southern Counties, 1825–1829;
Volume 7: Northern Counties, 1830–1834
Irma Harper and F. Edward Wright;
Volume 8: Southern Counties, 1830–1834

Maryland Eastern Shore Vital Records:
Book 1: 1648–1725, Second Edition; Book 2: 1726–1750; Book 3: 1751–1775;
Book 4: 1776–1800; and Book 5: 1801–1825

Maryland Militia in the War of 1812:
Volume 1: Eastern Shore; Volume 2: Baltimore City and County;
Volume 3: Cecil and Harford Counties; Volume 4: Anne Arundel and Calvert Counties;
Volume 5: St. Mary's and Charles Counties; Volume 6: Prince George's County;
and Volume 7: Montgomery County

Maryland Militia in the Revolutionary War
S. Eugene Clements and F. Edward Wright

Middlesex County Virginia, Marriage References and Family Relationships, 1673–1800

Middlesex County, New Jersey, Records of the 17th and 18th Centuries

New Castle County, Delaware, Marriage References and Family Relationships, 1680–1800

Newspaper Abstracts of Allegany and Washington Counties [Maryland], 1811–1815

Newspaper Abstracts of Cecil and Harford Counties [Maryland], 1822–1830

Newspaper Abstracts of Frederick County [Maryland], 1811–1815

Newspaper Abstracts of Frederick County [Maryland], 1816–1819

Northampton County, Virginia, Marriage References and Family Relationships, 1634–1800

Northumberland County, Virginia, Marriage References and Family Relationships, 1645–1800

Orphans' Court Proceedings of New Castle County, Delaware, 1742–1761

Quaker Minutes of the Eastern Shore of Maryland: 1676–1779

Quaker Records of Henrico Monthly Meeting and Other Church Records of Henrico, New Kent and Charles City Counties, Virginia

Quaker Records of South River Monthly Meeting, 1756–1800

Richmond County, Virginia, Marriage References and Family Relationships, 1692–1800

Sketches of Maryland Eastern Shoremen

St. Mary's County, Maryland, Marriage References and Family Relationships, 1634–1800

Stafford County, Virginia, Marriage References and Family Relationships, 1661–1800

Supplement to Maryland Eastern Shore Vital Records, Books 1–3

Sussex County, Delaware, Marriage References, 1648–1800

Sussex County, Delaware, Wills: 1800–1813

Tax List of Chester County, Pennsylvania, 1768

Tax List of York County, Pennsylvania, 1779

The Maryland Militia in the Revolutionary War
S. Eugene Clements and F. Edward Wright

Vital Records of Kent and Sussex Counties, Delaware, 1686–1800

Washington County [Maryland] Church Records of the 18th Century, 1768–1800

Western Maryland Newspaper Abstracts, Volume 1: 1786–1798

Western Maryland Newspaper Abstracts, Volume 2: 1799–1805

Western Maryland Newspaper Abstracts, Volume 3: 1806–1810

Wills of Chester County, Pennsylvania, 1766–1778

York County, Pennsylvania, Church Records of the 18th Century, Volume 1
Marlene S. Bates and F. Edward Wright

York County, Pennsylvania, Church Records of the 18th Century, Volume 2
Marlene Strawser Bates and F. Edward Wright

York County, Pennsylvania, Church Records of the 18th Century, Volume 3

York County, Virginia, Marriage References and Family Relationships, 1636–1800

York County, Virginia, Wills Inventories and Accounts, 1760–1783

www.ingramcontent.com/pod-product-compliance
Lightning Source LLC
LaVergne TN
LVHW050647100826
845148LV00011B/2016